Discovering
The Water of Leith

Discovering
The Water of Leith

HAMISH COGHILL

Maps by Brian Johnston

JOHN DONALD PUBLISHERS LTD
EDINBURGH

ISBN 0 85976 227 0

Phototypesetting by Newtext Composition Ltd., Glasgow.
Printed in Great Britain by Bell & Bain Ltd., Glasgow.

Acknowledgements

Many people have provided great encouragement and help along the way in the preparation of this book.

Every local writer appreciates the helpfulness of the staffs in the Edinburgh Room of our public library and in the National Library of Scotland.

My thanks to Ian Nimmo, Editor of the *Evening News,* for the use of photographs which have appeared in the paper, and to Brian Johnston for his artistic skills in the maps.

Especially I would like to express my appreciation to Mrs Mollie Tweedie for allowing me access to the manuscript on the Water of Leith prepared by her late husband – John Tweedie, Currie's local historian extraordinaire.

Finally, thanks to my family who kept me working at the book, and to John Tuckwell of John Donald, whose idea it was.

Contents

CHAPTER 1

'The Sound of Water and the Sound of Mills'

The Water of Leith weaves and bobs its way for more than eighteen miles from its gurgling source in the Colzium Springs on the north-western slopes of the Pentland Hills to its placid entry into the harbour of Leith at its journey's end.

But into that relatively short distance it has packed a tremendous vitality which has provided food, industry, jobs and now, more and more, the simple amenity for relaxation and enjoyment. Its scenery varies dramatically from moor land, through pleasant riverside meadows and deep gorges, and provides a constantly changing vista. The melting winter snows or heavy rains push up the water level very quickly, and turn a generally quiet-flowing stream into a chocolate torrent. Each season brings a difference to the view, literally day by day, and at every corner virtually you can find something of interest.

Nowadays there is a fine walkway stretching from its mouth to Balerno (with a few small gaps) and it has the great advantage of being easily accessible so that the walk can be tackled in easy stretches if the thought of a full river jaunt does not appeal.

The distinguished town planners Patrick Abercrombie and Derek Plumstead in their far-sighted (but alas too much neglected) plan for Edinburgh, published in 1949, realised the rich potential for recreational use. 'This offers one of the finest riverside walks that any citizen could ask for, but few, if any, of the citizens of Edinburgh know the full extent of the scenery that may be seen and enjoyed by following the course of this river from its mouth in Leith to the city boundary at Juniper Green and beyond. This is hardly surprising since the greater part of its banks lie within the property of many ownerships that bar the way to the public'.

Those words of forty years ago might have seemed prophetic, however, because Edinburgh Town Council and then the District Council, whose borders push far beyond Juniper Green, did decide to start a walkway in 1973 which with each additional segment has opened up the river to new

1

admirers. The Water of Leith, because of its passage, is frequently out of general view, but in so many places the casual viewer does get a glimpse of it – if only from the many bridges which pass over it. Many houses overlook the water, too, and the amount of riverside building in recent years has emphasised the attraction of such sites to developers. Indeed, a major problem may now well be to protect the remaining open spaces which still exist as haughs and smaller sites are eyed up for their building potential alone.

The walkway and therefore the river is enjoyed by walkers and joggers, cyclists and picnickers, artists and fishers – and marred by the canine and human vandals, the latter using the stream to dispose of rubbish of all sorts. The natural debris of a river gathers on the mill dams and on the banks waiting for a flush of high water to move it on, but tyres and old prams, plastic bottles and all sorts of household clutter hurled deliberately and possibly thoughtlessly into the river only mar the scene. And the Water of Leith Walkway Trust and others periodically organise clean-up drives to tidy a stretch of water, only to find the mindless rubbish quickly returns. But the Water has always suffered from this sort of thing.

The river has altered over the centuries – we know there were mills along its banks in at least the twelfth century – and there would certainly be small communities huddled there long before that. All down the Water you can see the influence of man seeking to control and use its flow, high old stone walls, lades, ruins, and some splendid former mills turned into dramatic homes.

What, then, is this stream acknowledged as being in its time one of the busiest in Scotland? Its known history extends over more than 900 years now, and its contribution to the development of the old towns of Edinburgh and Leith is inestimable.

The Rev. Dr John Walker, writing about the parish of Collington in the Statistical Account of Scotland in 1795, describes the Water of Leith: 'This small river does more work than perhaps any other, even of the largest size in Scotland'.

Later the Rev. Dr Lewis Balfour, grandfather of Robert Louis Stevenson, and parish minister at Colinton, says: 'The Water of Leith is a most serviceable drudge, and is by no means spared'.

On the rural stretch between Harperrigg Reservoir and Balerno, the Water of Leith is only a few feet wide. But in flood the waters quickly rise and the Haughhead ford now has a concrete base. The old bridge for pedestrians is no longer there, but the road ahead takes the walker into the Pentlands.

It is not the intention in this narrative to list the history of every building which used the Water as a source of power, the mills and other plants whose marks are seen on a walk along the banks. Some mills are readily recognisable, turned to different commercial uses or into housing; some are a rubble of stones with perhaps the trace of a lade or the old dam; others are now but names on an old map. But extant or extinct, these mills played a tremendous role in the communities clustered round the Water which they served in many ways. Basically the mills were started to grind oats to provide meal. Then came the luxuries after the basics – paper, spices, snuff, linen, glue. The history of the Water becomes a lineage of Scottish industrial and domestic development.

'Everywhere in this enchanted vale is the sound of water and the sound of mills – the wheel and the dam singing their alternative strain,' writes Stevenson, more specifically on the scene near his grandfather's manse. But the sound of water and the sound of mills have echoed down the valley of the Water of Leith since King David I in 1128 granted to the monks of Holyrood 'one of my mills of Dene' and 'a tithe of the new mill of Edinburgh'.

He also gave the monks the right to the mills near Broughton, resulting in the name of Canon Mills.

There is a deed of King Alexander II between Thomas of Lastalric on the one part and Master Ricard, parson of Halis (one of the old names of Colinton), concerning the mill dam of Halis which it was agreed would not be extended towards the church.

The Rev. William Lockhart, minister of Colinton Parish Church, says that at that time in 1226 there were 'scenes of industry towards the south-west (of the city) on the banks of the Water of Leith or the Water of the Hollow, for that seems to be the meaning of Leith, or Leth or Led as it is sometimes called. The mills were in all probability grain mills and their existence proves that the art of husbandry or agriculture was being pursued by the people in this neighbourhood at that time'.

By 1792 there was a grand total of 76 water-driven mills on the river, broken down as follows: 24 flour, 14 oatmeal, 12 barley, 7 saw, 6 snuff, 5 cloth fulling, 4 paper, 2 lint and 2 leather.

Henry Dempster, in a 'statistical account of mills and other public works' in 1854, lists 62 water wheels stretching from Leithhead to Leith saw mills, together with Balerno Bank paper mill and Hay's spinning mill on the Bevilaw (Bavelaw) Burn, the main tributary from the compensation reservoirs above Balerno. He says, too, there are six skinners, four tanners, one glue-work, and two distillers, 'one of which is now discontinued'. Other reports have put the number as high as more than 80 at one time.

Some of the mills belonged to the town of Edinburgh, and by the early eighteenth century they were returning an annual rent to the town council of more than 10,000 merks. As we will see when we look at the particular section of the river, trade incorporations of the old town held considerable sway over the

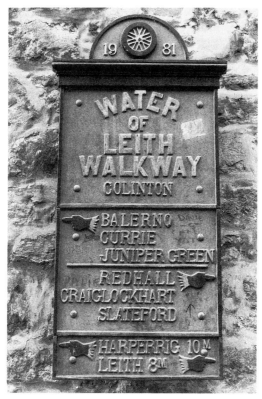

The well-signposted Water of Leith walkway stretches from Balerno to Leith Harbour. It is easily accessible at many points, and has now become a much appreciated feature all down the river's run. 'One of the finest riverside walks that any citizen could ask for,' planners Abercrombie and Plumstead forecast in their 1949 report.

mills, the Baxters (bakers) for instance being particularly involved in the Water of Leith Village (now Dean) and Canonmills.

The weavers, bonnetmen and skinners had close links with the waulk mills, and the mills in the country, as so many were in their day, relied on business from the town to keep them going.

Round the mills grew up the communities, once isolated villages like Balerno, Currie, Colinton, Coltbridge and so on, but now absorbed into the expanded Edinburgh.

The first paper mill on the Water seems to have been at Dalry where paper was being produced as early as 1591 by Mungo Russell and his son Gideon who employed two German craftsmen brought over by King James VI. The Russells had converted their small mill to papermaking, and in 1596 the Russells leased their paper mill to the Germans. Another of the early paper mills was founded at Canonmills about 1652 while another similar mill was noted at Spylaw by 1661.

The growth of the paper mills coincided with the growth of the newspaper and printing industry in Edinburgh. William Creech, a Lord Provost, bookseller and literary man, states that in 1763 there were three paper mills in the neighbourhood of the town, and in 1790 the figure was twelve. 'And a vast quantity of printing paper was sent to London, from whence it used formerly to be brought. Some of these paper mills are upon a more extensive scale than any in Britain.' In those days paper used for the various journals had to be sent to London to be stamped for excise duty. Between 1763 and 1790 the number of printing houses in the town, incidentally, grew from six to sixteen.

One of the most intriguing names of all the mills is Jinkabout, which stood on the north bank between Bogsmill and Slateford. It too was a paper mill and was leased in 1714 by John Reid, proprietor of the *Edinburgh Gazette*. Reid was imprisoned for infringing the monopoly of the King's printer Mrs Agnes Campbell.

In 1586, Jinkabout, which stood where the walled garden of the old Redhall House now is, was Lumsdaine's corn mill, and later a barley mill. Such changes in the use of mills was very common, and not many remained in one use during their lifetime – from paper to glue to tannery (Balerno) or lint to meal to snuff (Kirkland Mills at Colinton) are typical examples as new proprietors took over and saw a way to make a living from meeting new demands.

At Bogsmill, below Colinton, in 1735 the Bank of Scotland had their bank notes manufactured. There is record of a barber coming twice from Edinburgh to shave officials – he received a 3s fee. The bank also appears to have kept all the employees in food while the note paper was being produced. A man was employed for twelve days cutting meat – 200lbs of it

Journey's end and an old windlass at Sandport marks the meeting of the freshwater river and the salt water at the docks. Close by the Sandport stands Leith's handsome Custom House, designed by Robert Reid and built between 1810-12.

at a cost of 2½d a lb for meat and mutton. A hen cost 8d, a duck 9d, a 'sollan gouss' 1s 4d, wild fowl 10d. The officials and workers certainly lived high on the hog!

At the back of Spylaw House at Colinton stands the old snuff mill which provided the money to found one of Edinburgh's best-known hospitals and later schools – James Gillespie's. James and his brother John built up a very successful business with James a character who carried the snuff on his back into their High Street shop. As Gillespie prospered, he bought a horse carriage and Henry Erskine is attributed with drafting the lines:

> Wha wad hae thocht it,
> That noses had bocht it,

when Gillespie asked him for a motto for its side.

Snuff-milling is referred to from the 1740s and the Water of Leith was one of the most prosperous in Scotland for this trade. In the 1850s there were still five snuff mills around Colinton, and the last mill, Watt's at Juniper Green, closed only early in the Second World War. The water level in many places was higher than it is now – there are even references to the 'great river' – and the banks were also the site of bleachfields, particularly at Inglis Green which was started in 1773 by George Inglis and Joseph Reid. They advertised, 'having fitted up all conveniences necessary for carrying on the printing business and having a choice collection of the most fashionable patterns . . . are to print all kinds of linen and cotton'.

There were printfields at Gorgie and Bonnington, and in the 1760s there was a proposal for a water-powered thread-twisting machine at Bonnington, a move which the proprietor believed would have ousted all the thread makers in Midlothian. Bonnington was also the site wanted in 1711 by the sail cloth manufacturers for beating mills, workshops and bleachfields for hemp. Whether the plan was carried out in full is not certain, although Edinburgh Town Council gave a 38-year tack on the mills. One of the most interesting, if short-lived, industries came with the granting of a tack to Richardson Terrand and Micah Shields to erect smelt mines and make dams and sluices for copper mining at Currie. At the expiry of their tack in 1758 the speculators appeared to have run out of funds, and the copper seems to have been insignificant. The coming of the mills did mean the passing of some of the cottage industry which earned a few coppers for the participants. Dr Balfour, for instance, laments in 1845 that 'spinning has almost disappeared'.

'Thus the old are cut off from the employment, within the power of age and suited to its disposition, of 'drawing out a thread wi' little din;' which used to keep time from being a burden, and to supply with the necessaries of life.'

The preponderance of mills and their inevitable effluent pouring downstream from Balerno affected the quality of the water which would be used for drinking, cooking, washing and other purposes, this in addition to all sorts of sewage that found its way into it.

In 1617 the Scots Parliament could set as a measure a 'pinct stoup' containing the 'weight of Thrie Pounds seven unces of frensh Troys weght cleare runing water of the Watter of Leith'.

Many mills have been damaged by flood, and in September 1659 eleven of the town mills and five owned by Heriot's Hospital were destroyed in a tumultuous storm just after the Town Council put a tax on ale. The diarist John Nicoll records: 'The Lord did manifest his anger . . .'

Thus, with a sense of history, our footsteps turn to discovering something of the Water's tale.

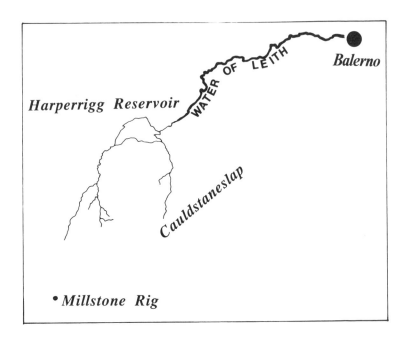

CHAPTER 2
Harperrig to Balerno

The Water of Leith starts in the part of the Pentland Hills known as Millstone Rig, and runs past the remains of Cairns Castle and into Harperrigg Reservoir, one of the group built to compensate the mills downstream for the loss of water when the North Pentland Water scheme came into being and tapped springs to provide the growing city of Edinburgh with fresh supplies.

One of the important drove roads of Central Scotland crossed over the Water a short way from the eastern end of the reservoir, below the East and West Cairn hills, and sliced through the Pentlands – the Cauldstane Slap. As late as the end of last century cattle were still being taken along this route.

A.B. Haldane relates in his account of droving in Scotland: 'The cattle 'stanced' for the night in the meadow or beside the drove road all up the slope of the Pentland Hills towards the pass, the drovers sleeping beside them, the 'topsmen' or the owners sleeping in the farmhouse'. The cattle were traditionally taken from the Falkirk Tryst over the hills into Peeblesshire and on to markets in England.

Running to the north of the stream at this point is the Lang Whang, the Balerno to Carnwath stretch of the Lanark Road. At the beginning of the nineteenth century three coaches a week left the Grassmarket in the heart of Edinburgh for Lanark. The names along the way were well-known to the passengers on their bumpy trip – Boll of Bere farm, House on the Muir, Little Vantage, Cairns Castle Inn, all before the horse-changing point at Tabrax. The drove road passed to the west of the old toll house at Little Vantage, and a short distance away stood the old inn of the same name, with the driveway still traceable. The Slap, which became known as the Thieves' Road because of freebooters swooping on the cattlemen, had a self-appointed guardian at one time in Sir George Crighton, High Admiral of Scotland, who possessed Cairns Castle and also built Blackness Castle on the shores of the Forth. Cairns Castle itself was certainly in the possession of William de Carnys in 1349.

11

Silent guardian at the western end of Harperrig Reservoir stands the ruined Cairns Castle, home at one time of Sir George Crighton, the self-appointed guardian of the Cauldstane Slap – the drovers' pass through the Pentlands.

Back on the waterside is the little community of Leithhead Farm, not far from the approach to the Slap. At Leithhead, or Leithshead as it was originally known in records of 1662, were the mills which tapped first the driving force of the Water of Leith on its run. Two mills ground corn or barley, and coarse

Now a huddle of houses, the Leithhead community because of its location was the first on the Water of Leith to use its power for their milling. It was a classic example of how the water could be tapped and put to industrial as well as farming use.

paper was also produced there. A diversion pipe from the lade took water to a threshing mill, and also drove a wheel to power a churn – waste not, want not indeed.

As John Tweedie, Currie's local historian, has observed: 'Four hundred years ago this Water of Leith was peopled by typical farm villagers – groups of people who lived in self-supporting communities and who rarely moved. All their basic needs were supplied on the farm. Each man worked according to his skill, but each man's work contributed to the benefit of all. The landowner's dues were met in kind, and his responsibilities were clear. As a holder of land he had to supply a mill, a brewery and a place of worship. Agricultural and communal agreements were made at the Burlaw Court, and the Kirk Session looked after the moral welfare of the community, the needs of the poor, and in later years the education of the parish'.

It's still very much countryside as the Water reaches Glenbrook upstream from Balerno.

The river is in rich farmland at this stage – there are still fords below Sunnyside and at Haughhead – and the estate of Cockburn covered a large part of the ground on the south bank. Cockburn House, where a dairy business is now based, dates to 1672, but in the fifteenth century the estate was part of the Barony of Baulernoght (Balerno), and for many years it later belonged to the Edinburgh Merchant Company.

Like many great estates, however, parts have been sold over the years. Once a dominating feature, Kaimes Hill to the north is gradually vanishing under the impact of quarrying, while on the adjoining Dalmahoy Hill it is worth a scramble to see defence trenches and ramparts thrown up by ancient dwellers who would certainly have explored and used the riches the river could provide.

Balerno has seen many changes in recent years with major housing developments. However, these youngsters can still savour something of the old life in the pedestrianised main street of the old village.

At Whelpside Farm the character of the land changes and the river goes between higher banks as it starts its drop towards the city, reaching first of all Balerno.

A peaceful Midlothian village until the housing explosion of the early sixties changed it for ever, Balerno was originally a 'ferm toun' and its first expansion came with the paper mills in the late eighteenth and early nineteenth centuries, and a further influx came with the labouring force who built the Pentland reservoirs.

It is now a commuter community, the old village centre having been drastically reshaped over the past few years. New

Three little maids, ladies-in-waiting to the Balerno Gala Queen who is elected to preside at the annual gala. It's a happy week in which both incomers and older residents join with enthusiasm – and a reminder of the community's strong village independence.

housing sprawls over what was open countryside and fresh fields are eyed by developers anxious to take up the proven boom of a house in the country image.

Despite all the pressures on it, however, Balerno has managed to retain a proud independence exerted through its own community council, local newspaper, and the successful running of a Gala Week, complete with queen.

John Geddie, writing just before the turn of the century, describes the scene above Balerno Bridge: 'Country houses, surrounded by their woods and gardens are planted in glades by the water-side or occupy commanding sites on the banks above. . . .'

'The city is still seven or eight miles off. But the pretty Water of Leith railway to Balerno gives easy access to this charming district, neighbour to the hills, yet sheltered from the rougher winds by its trees and braes: and men who labour hard at the

Dusk over Threipmuir Reservoir lying beneath the Black Hill above Balerno. Many of the Irish labourers imported to construct the compensation ponds on the Pentlands settled in Balerno last century.

drudgery of commerce, law and journalism find here a delightful place of sojourn in the holiday months of summer and autumn, and an agreeable retreat all the year round from the cares of the week.'

At the old smiddy on Johnsburn Road there must have been some excitement the day John Aikman, one of its occupants, believed he had found the secret of flight. He carefully constructed wings over his forge and then clambered onto the roof of the smiddy – and proceeded to prove they did not work. His family and friends arranged for him to go into care after that.

Tucked away in the wood behind the smiddy building, but still discernible on close inspection, is the old curling pond gifted by a minister at Currie Kirk.

Another Balerno smith, Thomas Horsburgh, is believed to have invented the iron-shafted golf club, but as there was no interest at the time his patent lapsed and he lost out on a fortune.

17

Malleny House, partly seventeenth century, is now in the hands of the
National Trust for Scotland. And only four of the twelve magnificent
yew trees – called the Twelve Apostles – still stand in the lovely
gardens which are open to the public. The trees are said to have been
planted to mark the Union of Scotland and England. National Trust
photo.

Two men whose style enlivened the rural village, as did the
Irish labourers who worked on the construction of Threipmuir
and Harlaw reservoirs which trap the headwaters of the
Bavelaw Burn, the main tributary to our Water which it joins at
Balerno.

For those hard-working navvies the conditions of a country
bothy or farm cottage to lay a head and maybe raise a family
must have been far removed from those endured by their
countrymen forced into Edinburgh's slums during the building
of the Union Canal.

The first sod in that great engineering work was cut in
March 1818, to be completed in May 1822, starting at Port
Hopetoun in the city and ending at the Forth and Clyde Canal
31½ miles away near Falkirk.

The road through Balerno to the Bavelaw Ponds, passing the
nature reserve of the Red Moss at the end of Threipmuir, is

well known to walkers as a good gateway into the Pentlands.

Being a country area, Balerno – Byrney or Ballernoch on older maps – has many historical associations, with Ravelrig House, now a Dr Barnardo's home, being recorded in fifteenth-century documents, for instance. Its superiority in 1500 was granted by Archibald Wauchope to Sir William Werok of the chapel of Nudrie Merschale; it passed to the Ruthven family who had it confiscated for their part in the Gowrie conspiracy.

Connected with the Ravelrig estate in the mid-seventeenth century is an eminent Scottish surgeon, Arthur Temple, who performed one of the strangest operations of his time. Temple was admitted to the College of Surgeons in 1650 and twice served as its president, but the operation which brought him to wider public notice took place in 1671 when he removed a horn growing from a woman's head.

In the archives of Edinburgh University is a spiral horn with a silver plate reading: 'This horn was cut by Arthur Temple, chirgurgion, out of the head of Elizabeth Low being three inches above the right ear . . . It was agrowing 7 years, her age 50 yeares'. To the visitor the horn was one of the sights of the city at the time.

The variation on the name Balerno is typical of place names throughout the Lothians which have altered in spelling over the years. In 1280 Balhernoch is recorded – and it is suggested it comes from the Gaelic and means the place of the sloe bush or tree. The old Barony of Balerno covered Curriehill, Ravelrig, Harlaw, Cockburn and Leithhead, and the stent roll of 1478 mentions Cockburn, Baulernocht, Rawelek, Harlaw, Pilmuir and Bauleny, all still in existence.

Probably the best-known house now in the Balerno area is Malleny, owned by the National Trust for Scotland, and set in a most pleasing and colourful walled garden. The original part of the house was built in the seventeenth century, with a later extension, and in the garden are four yew trees – the last of what were known as the Twelve Apostles, reputedly planted to celebrate the Union of Scotland and England.

The recent formation of the Friends of Malleny has encouraged a wider use of the garden. Down the side of the garden cascades the Bavelaw Burn which brought to the village its Malleny waulk mill, Byrnie's paper and sawmills, of which nothing remains – sheltered housing covers its site – and the Balerno Bank mill of 1805.

The grain wheels at Newmills crushed the corn for the villagers in 1604 and the ruins sit within the garden of Old Millhouse, a few yards down the Water of Leith walkway which starts beside the new high school, and follows the old railway line. The Balerno Express, as locals called it, ran for the last time in 1943, although commercial traffic ran until 1968, and the station site was on the north side of Lanark Road, now covered by a garden.

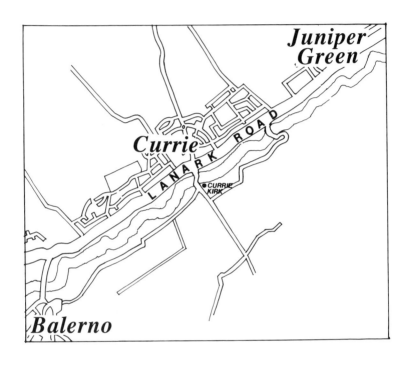

CHAPTER 3
Currie and Juniper Green

The walkway now is a steady, level footing, but for the occupant of Newmills in 1889 there was certainly a feeling of uneasiness for a few moments as the ground tilted beneath him. 'James Robertson, Newmills, was seated in an armchair after breakfast . . . the chair moved forward twice as if someone pushed it upwards momentarily . . . and a tin tray rattled against the wall,' said *The Scotsman* of January 19th. This was the earth tremor which shook a house in Blinkbonny Village and stopped Currie Kirk clock at 'between 10 and 5 minutes to 7'.

As the walkway progresses, clear signs of milling history unfold in a very pleasant stretch of the Water. The piggery was originally a waulk mill or 'fulling mill of Ballernock' as it is described in a 1376 charter. Fulling was the treatment of woven cloth in water to shrink and tighten the weave which in early days was done by feet, hence waulking. The huge former Balerno Paper Mill is now a tannery, and the building stands on the site of an earlier mill.

The Balerno Mill had a link with the Edinburgh stationers Waverley Cameron whose predecessors MacNiven and Cameron had their paper produced there from 1788. In that year they advertised the opening of their premises in Blair Street 'for the sale of paper of their own manufacture'. And the company are still in Blair Street with their famous advertising slogan: 'They come as a boon and a blessing to men, the Pickwick, the Owl and the Waverley Pen'.

The village of Currie is now also swamped by modern housing and drastic road widening to cope with the heavy traffic flow, but the centre is clearly retained round the Kirk, the bridge and some of the older buildings which line the main road.

Currie was originally known as Killeith, or one of its variations such as Kildeleith. The name means the chapel by the Leith and the original parish church was dedicated to St Kentigern or St Mungo. A little spring down by the waterside

The familiar signs in Blair Street, off Edinburgh's Royal Mile. MacNiven and Cameron, now Waverley Cameron, had their paper produced in Balerno Mill from 1788, the year they advertised the opening of their Blair Street warehouse.

below Currie Brig is known as St Mungo's well.

The Kirk of Currie has always been recognised as being 'of ane speciall rectorie and personage apperteining to the Archedeane of Louthione'. The founding date is uncertain but there is reference to Robert de Keldeleth, the monk who became abbot of the Benedictine monastery of Dunfermline about 1240. Later he was Chancellor of Scotland and keeper of the Great Seal. The name De Curry or De Curri, according to R.B. Langwill, historian and son of a Currie parish minister, was not uncommon in the twelfth and thirteenth centuries, occurring frequently in documents and charters, and in 1368 there is a reference to the 'barony of Curry in the county of Edinburgh'.

At the time of the Reformation there was perhaps an understandable reluctance of some of the parishioners to accept the new type of Presbyterian worship. In 1564 the

General Assembly of the Church of Scotland had to call down civil punishment on 'sic as hes steiked the doors of the paroche kirk, and will not open the same to parochiners that presented themselves to have heard the word of God preached'.

This was necessary in five parishes, one of them being Currie. The first Protestant minister in 1568 was Adam Letham or Lichtoun, who was succeeded in 1591 by his son, Matthew.

The people of Currie were among those who were urged by Archibald Johnston of Warriston, one of the leading figures in the Covenant, to support the great national movement in 1638. He had bought his estate in the parish of Currie a few years earlier, and his diary for March 18, 1638, records the following description of the scene in Currie Kirk:

'Being a solemne fast day apoynted for subscription of the Covenant, he (the minister 'Jhon Chairtres') read it al over again as he had doone the Sunday of befoir; he syne explained to the people all the pairts of it. Theirafter, to schau his warrand for seiking, and thairs for giving, ane oath at the renovation of the Covenant, he pressed the 10ch Nehem v 28 and 29 . . . and the 2 Chron ch 15 v 12 . . . quhairof applyed verry weal every word. Yet in al this tyme thair was no motion nor tears in any of the congregation; bot immediately thairafter at his lifting up of his hand, and his desyring the congregation to stand up and lift up their hands and sueare unto the aeternal God, and at their standing up and lifting up their hands, in the tuinkling of ane eye their fell sutch ane extraordinaire influence of Gods Spirit upon the whol congregation, melting their frozen hearts, waltering thair dry cheeks, chainging thair verry countenances, as it was a wonder to seie so visible, sensible, momentaneal a chainge upon al, man and woman, lasse and ladde, pastor and people, that Mr Jhon, being sufficat almost with his auin tears, and astonisched at the motion of the whol people, sat doune in the pulpit in ane amazement . . .'

For his Covenanting enthusiasm Mr Jhon was imprisoned on the Bass Rock, and in due course Lord Warriston himself was executed at the instigation of King Charles II on the Restoration.

The present church, which is beautifully situated on the

Young men and women still try out their climbing skills where one of the world's leading mountaineers, Dougal Haston, practised his first climbs on the wall alongside the walkway near Currie. Haston died in an avalanche in Switzerland and his Currie connections are recorded on a stone outside the local post office.

ancient grounds on the south side of the river, was built in 1785. The previous year the heritors, or local landowners, decided a new church should be built, and in the *Edinburgh Advertiser* of September 14th that year interested parties could read the following advertisement: 'A New Kirk, 55 feet long, by 34 feet wide, to be built at Currie, six miles west from Edinburgh. Plans and Estimates will be taken into consideration at a meeting of the Heritors to be held at Currie, on Saturday the 9th day of October next, at 12 o'clock midday. A small reward to be given to him only whose plan shall be adopted. Undertakers will see the conditions of contract, in the hands of the Rev Mr James Craig minister, or Mr Taylor schoolmaster there. Not to be repeated'.

The plan put forward by Mr James Thomson was duly accepted. To the east of the church itself stands the session house incorporating the remains of an ancient 'quire'. This building has thirteenth-century arches in its south wall, and during the conversion many Celtic stones were found. Two calvary stones found while digging a grave are also displayed in the interior back wall of the church.

The completion of the new building, to which the clock was added in 1818, enthused the dominie William Taylor, a poet of some distinction, to versify:

> An' Currie Kirk, of area wide,
> An' splendid waws, erect an' high,
> Wi' spacious roof, of Esdale pride,
> An' steeple tow'rin to the sky,
> Attracts the fancy of a' those
> Who pass the Parish thorow;
> Frae Forth to Tweed, in ony Town,
> Forsooth it has nae marrow.

One of the interesting pieces of church equipment was a sand glass which was purchased so that the preacher (and presumably the long-suffering congregation) could see the length of the sermon carefully measured. James Nicoll, the church officer, was ordered in June 1699 to procure the glass 'to be set up to those who preach', and in the parish accounts there are payments 'for a Sandglass to the Church' and 'to James Ffinny for minding ye iron yt holdeth ye Sandglass'.

The parish had a happy record of longevity, and the Statistical Account of Scotland records that William Napier, a day labourer, had died 'at the advanced age of 113, and till a few years, 5 or 6 at most, before his death, he followed his usual employment'.

'At present there is alive one William Ritchie, a farmer, who is 105 years old, and, what is singular in the history of this man, he incurred the censure of the church, for his connections with the sex, after he had attained the 90th year of his age.' Something in the country air, indeed.

The New Statistical Account of 1845 notes that Ritchie had died at the age of 108 and his son Adam 'exceeded the age of

The imposing ruin of Lennox Tower looms over the Water. The subject of much speculation as to its origins, the Tower now lies within the grounds of a private house, but was in its day a strong-point on the river bank.

100'. Dr William Nisbet, physician in Edinburgh, who wrote the first account of the parish, has some telling words on the character of the people of the late eighteenth century – 'Till within these few years, the people of the parish were sober, industrious, and economical. The vices of the capital, however, are beginning to spread fast amongst them, and the introduction of those baneful articles to the poor, tea and whisky, will soon produce that corruption of morals and debility of constitution, which are already so severely felt in many parishes, and which must soon materially injure the real strength and population of Scotland. The introduction of these articles, is one bad effect of the present practice of debasing and vitiating malt liquor. Formerly, when that liquor (ale) was the only beverage in use, excesses from it did not affect the constitution, as it contained a good deal of nourishment. But now, since it has been debased, it is entirely given up. Tea, as a dietetic article, is substituted in its place, and it is not uncommon to see a labouring man here dining upon it.'

The later Account gives us a very good impression of what living conditions were like – the average wage for hinds hired annually for farm work amounting, together with a house and garden allowance, to £26, while 'common agricultural day-labourers' received 10s a week. Women fit for field work were hired at 10d a day, and children at 8d, 'without victuals'.

Those working in the mills included many women, and children under the age of 14 who were employed picking rags and finishing paper. During the early years of last century, the bodysnatchers operated their grisly trade to supply bodies to the medical men whose then bizarre surgical lessons for their students opened up new frontiers. In 1821 Currie village was rocked by its own involvement in such an adventure. A cart apparently loaded with peat was being driven by two men down the road from Lanark towards the city when it was spotted by two workmen breaking stones. They thought the cart was lightly loaded and suspected the peats were only a covering for something below. They ran to James Craig, overseer of Balerno Paper Mill, and by chance the excise officer William Elliot was at the mill. He went to stop the cart and discovered the bodies of a man and woman hidden beneath the peat. The cart drivers Andrew Miller and Thomas Hidge were taken into custody and duly sent for trial at the High Court in Edinburgh, charged with violating the sepulchres of the dead in the churchyard in Lanark. They were both found guilty and given six months' imprisonment. In the meantime, three persons from Currie had been deputed to take the bodies back for reburial at Lanark where they were treated 'to an excellent and plentiful dinner'.

The local poet James Thomson of Kinleith published a 6d pamphlet shortly after the incident: 'A Poem, Chiefly in the Scottish Dialect, on Raising and Selling the Dead'. In it he praised the courage of the good officer Elliot, and summed up his feelings thus:

Currie Community Council have won the right to recreate the old Fair Week and Riding of the Marches after an absence of about a century. The council were the first in Scotland to be granted their own coat of arms which council secretary Donald Cruickshank (left) and Russell Thomson, of the council's planning committee, show. The 'new' Riding is scheduled for 1989.

> Of a' the articles for sale,
> Whilk bodies think is lawfu',
> To sell the dead, it bangs the hale –
> There's something in't that's awfu'!

A few years earlier in 1818 Currie Kirk itself had been involved in a case of bodysnatching. In the parish records there is an entry: 'By searching for a dead woman stolen from churchyard, 2/6d'. In June of that year the Kirk Session and heritors considered a petition asking for a watch-house to be built in the churchyard as a precaution against the resurrectionists. The subsequent watch-house stood until 1884 when it was removed to make way for an extension of the burial ground.

The nineteenth-century Currie centred round the Kirk at the far end of the bridge. The remains of the kiln can still be seen but the miller's house and cottages have long since gone. Over the bridge 'Bloody Tam' Dalyell led his troopers to tackle the Covenanters at Rullion Green.

One of the oldest remains in Currie is the kiln which stands at the north side of the bridge, beside the remnants of Currie Mill. The miller's thatched house was destroyed by fire in the 1940s and a character who operated at the bridge is also recorded in a Thomson poem:

> At Currie brig-end, auld Marion was kend,
> For forty years at least, by the great and the sma',
> The ragget an' braw, the dominie, elder and priest . . .
> Whar will ye now get pint or gill,
> When Marion's dead?

There is reference to repairs to the arched bridge in the Kirk Session records in 1599, and there is a saying 'as deep as Currie brig', indicating not only shrewdness but selfish cunning according to one commentator.

Originally the largest paper-making unit on the river, Kinleith Mill site is now an industrial complex. It had a 150-feet-high chimney, a local landmark, and when the foundations for it were dug, Bronze Age relics were found.

It is fitting in a community so accustomed to the clank of the mill wheel that the poet should find time to pen a few lines to the millmaster John Stein, who was a subscriber to his book of poetry:

> Lang may your mill keep haill an' weel,
> May naething skaith her outer wheel,
> Nae bits o' flint, nor things o' steel,
>   Gang through the happer,
> To spoil the stanes, an' gar them reel,
>   An' stop the clapper.

One of the mysteries of this stretch of the Water centres on the ruin of Lennox Tower standing in the grounds of Lymphoy House on the high northern bank. It is suggested it was built by the Earl of Lennox, Darnley's brother, although no charter dates the Lennox family to the lands until 1593. Before that date the tower was known as Killeith. It seems Mary,

There's plenty of fun in the annual Water of Leith pram race for charity. The Railway Inn at Juniper Green was the starting point for this happy group in 1988.

Queen of Scots stayed in the tower which shows traces in its ruined state of having been a formidable and comfortable building.

John Tweedie suggests that the tower could originally have been the 'special manssioun' seat of the Archdeans of Lothian who are listed in the vestibule of Currie Kirk.

As with so many old buildings, legends abound, including the tale of the piper who tried to explore a subterranean tunnel from the tower; the sound of his pipes was followed to Currie Brig where he vanished. (But then there's another story that a similar tunnel runs from Edinburgh Castle down the Royal Mile and a piper vanished there too! Piping must have been a risky business!)

Down river from Currie Kirk, now a small industrial estate and potential housing area, stands what was the Kinleith Paper Mill, the largest mill on the Water. Bronze Age relics were discovered during building operations last century, together

Every year restocking of the Water with trout provides anglers with good sport. With the control of pollution, fishermen can try their luck on most stretches under the watchful eyes of the Water Bailiffs.

with a stone kist burial ground. The mill at Killeithe is mentioned in 1618 and mills existed there throughout the seventeenth and eighteenth centuries. But it was in 1844 that the Kinleith Mill was greatly expanded by Henry Bruce, particularly with the development of steam power. The mill even made its own gas, and Currie street lighting was run off this supply for many years. The mill's most prominent feature was a 280-feet high chimney built in 1878 to eliminate pollution.

It was demolished some years ago, and other demolitions of parts of the mill complex leave only a reminder of what a bustling place Kinleith Mill, which closed in 1966, was in its heyday.

In the late 1700s the Currie mills were handling barley to supply the Glasgow market. Part of the load was sent to the West Indies 'where it serves for food for the negroes, being preferred by some to rice'. The carts taking the barley to the west returned laden with rum and sugar for the Edinburgh markets – 'A single horse, in this trade, will transport often near a ton weight: a strong proof of the goodness of the turnpike roads in this quarter,' adds Dr Nisbet.

The independence of the old village life has been recaptured recently. Currie Community Council, a very go-ahead group, have won the right to stage the traditional Riding of the parish boundary, the formal 'staking out' of the land. In 1987 they were also successful in having assigned to them the rights and privileges of former landowners – granted by the Scots Parliament in 1705 – to hold two fairs annually.

The Council were the first in Scotland to be granted their own coat of arms, and the bearings boast the motto 'Aye Spier An Rede Weel' – 'Always inquire and counsel (or guard) well'.

Above the walkway on the northern slope is Juniper Green – the name first appears in 1707 – which formerly stood on the old Curriemuirend and was a village which developed with the coming of industry in the valley. Its name possibly came from the junipers and whins which covered the land at that point.

'Hither flock the summer lodgers in their season,' reports John Geddie in 1896, 'and townspeople find Juniper Green a pleasant and acceptable retreat all the year round. It has reminiscences of De Quincey and Christopher North . . . But none of its guests are likely to shed more lustre on it than the Carlyles, who came hither in their early house-keeping days.' Thomas and Jane Carlyle spent their early married days in a house in Comely Bank, then on the outskirts of Edinburgh.

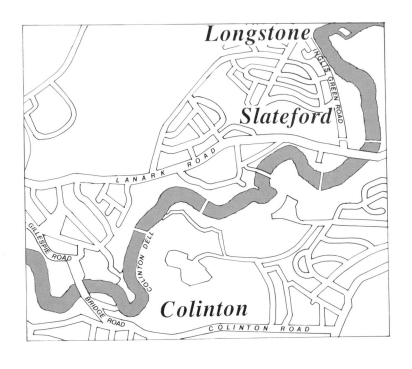

CHAPTER 4

Colinton to Slateford

One of the first traces of Colinton is found around 1095 through the old name of Hale (in its various forms of Hala, Hales, Hailes, Halis, Halys, Heallis) – now generally known as Hailes. It came in the gifts of land from Ethelred, second son of Malcolm Canmore and Queen Margaret, to the Church of the Holy Trinity at Dunfermline. The name Hailes was used for the parish for hundreds of years, and the original church building was on a site east of Hailes mansion, near the present Lanark Road.

The Rev. William Lockhart suggests that the origins of the church may stretch back further than the eleventh century because St Cuthbert was the patron saint, and may have left his cell in Lindisfarne to visit the then remote district of Lothian.

The town of Hales is mentioned in a letter from Pope Gregory IX in August 1292. We also know that in 1226 there was a dispute over the boundaries of a mill and the land surrounding it, the property of Thomas of Lastalric and the rector of the parish.

'There was also in the same year a mill called 'Dregern' mill, which was teined, and in a dispute which arose between the brethren of St Leonard's Hospital, Edinburgh, and the parson of the parish, the acting mandatories of the Pope gave the teinds to the brethren of St Leonard's, but ordained them to pay to the church of Hailes three shillings, viz: eighteen pence at Pentecost (Whit Sunday) and eighteen pence at the feast of St Martin (Martinmas) for providing lights for that church,' says Mr Lockhart.

Hale is a Celtic word meaning moor or hillock, and in the plural probably described the rolling moorland before man made his impression. Of the original church there is little trace, and the present church was built in 1771 – 'a very decent and convenient structure for public worship,' according to Dr John Walker in the Statistical Account. 'Though plain, and executed at a very moderate expense, it is rather elegant, both on the outside and inside. It has even served as a model for some

FORMERLY
THE SHOP OF
JAMES GILLESPIE
OF SPYLAW
TOBACCO AND SNUFF
MANUFACTURER
FOUNDER OF
JAMES GILLESPIE'S
HOSPITAL
AND SCHOOLS
DIED 8 APRIL 1797
ERECTED BY
THE GOVERNORS 198?

With a nose like that there's little doubting James Gillespie's trade – snuff! The plaque in the High Street in Edinburgh marks the shop where the snuff ground at their Spylaw Mill was sold to the Edinburgh populace in the eighteenth century by the Gillespie brothers.

parish churches that have since been built.'

The manse, he adds, was built in 1784 'at an expense sufficiently liberal, but with very inefficient workmanship. That is the case with the generality of the manses in Scotland, and which renders them, in proportion to their size, the most expensive in Scotland'. How many parish ministers have echoed that view of their large, draughty houses!

Dr Walker was known as the 'mad minister of Moffat' because of his great interest in botany – he became the first Professor of Natural History at Edinburgh University. He is said to have been particularly obsessed with the appearance of his wig, and so immaculate were the curls that the ladies in his congregation were sure the insect net which stuck out from his pocket during his walks was really a pair of curling tongs.

Stevenson, as we have seen, never forgot his boyhood days spent in the manse garden at Colinton with his maternal grandfather Dr Balfour. In the 1845 New Statistical Account Dr Balfour comments: 'There are no customs peculiar to the parish. The people are on the whole attentive to cleanliness, dress well on the Sabbath, and, if they would act aright, have the comforts and advantages of society in a 'reasonable degree'.'

'They are not generally given to reading. Some years ago an attempt was made to cherish the practice, by introducing among them itinerant libraries – the first year's expense having been kindly defrayed by a friend. But the experiment came to a close at the end of the fourth year, when the money drawn from the readers was not equal to the hire of the books.'

'One vice prevails greatly among the people, which eats out a man's heart and renders him indifferent to religion, to knowledge, and to his nearest and dearest friends, viz, the drinking of ardent spirits. It was ascertained that the drinking portion of the working classes must have spent £2300 for spirits in 1834. How ruinous is that appetite which withdraws so large a sum in so small a society from ministering to its comfort and improvement.'

A temperance society was formed in the village, but after an early enthusiasm its influence apparently waned.

The parish church has a good record for looking after the unfortunates within its boundaries. In 1698, for instance, a weekly ration of one peck of oatmeal was given to those on the poor roll, the heritors meeting half the cost and the chief tenants the balance. The records from 1714-1720 include such donations as 'To Mary Corbet a miserable object being both deaf and dumb' 6s; to Mrs Jardine, a cripple gentlewoman and for a horse to carry her to Currie 5s; to Hugh Pennington 'who being sometimes a mariner had his tongue cut out and cruelly used by barbarous persons' 3s.

While the benevolence flowed, the penalties for transgressing the Kirk's set way of life could be pretty hard. Swearing or any arguing on the post-Reformation Sabbath was a terrible offence. Jean Jackson of Bonaly was ordered to 'make publique

Another stage in the walkway completed – in 1981 the new bridge over the Water in Spylaw Park was completed, and Charlotte Cottingham, the landscape architect, had every reason to be happy about the outcome of the work.

ucknowledgment of sorrow for her sin next Lord's Day'. The following year, 1652, a parishioner John Millar was hauled before the Kirk Session for his profanity in not coming to Sunday service 'as he had companie from Edinburgh but did not drink'.

The Kirk officer was paid 2s 'for everie person he shall cite to the Sessions' – he must have been a popular man.

The public confession of 'sins', the punishment of standing in a sack cloth at the church door, doubtless the subject of sanctimonious tongues, of being locked into the iron 'jougs' or forced to sit on the cutty stane, often for weeks of public humiliation, was generally accepted with little question.

Colinton was very much an isolated, rural community, thinly populated, and in 1709 the parish contained not many more than 400 souls. But in 1774 Dr Walker can relate: 'The numerous mills erected for flour and barley; the mills for the manufacture of flax, paper, tobacco, and the waulking of cloth; the skinnery manufacture; the bleaching fields; a flourishing distillery; a manufacture of magnesia; and the great quarries of Hailes and Redhall; have brought together, of late years, into this parish, a concourse of people, and a degree of opulence formerly unknown'.

Dr Balfour more than sixty years on reflects the growing affluence in this account: 'The cultivation of the parish, since the last Statistical Account was written, has been greatly improved, and is generally carried on with activity and intelligence. Considerable changes have taken place in the various manufactures then existing in the parish. The distillery has disappeared; the skinnery! its very name is lost, having given place to the more poetical designation of Laverock dale; the magnesia manufactory is in ruins; the noise of the waulk-mill no longer reminds the passenger of its existence; and the mill, for beating flax is, comparatively speaking, in little use. Still the parish flourishes; the population has increased; the rental has improved; and could a little more of that right-hearted prudence which inclines, and, through God's blessing, enables man to value and steadily comply with the counsels of heavenly truth, be infused into the bosom of the generality of the people, they would be blessed indeed'.

A grim reminder of the bodysnatchers lies in the grounds of St Cuthbert's Parish Church at Colinton. The mort safe is 7 feet long, 2 feet 6 inches wide, and 1 foot 6 inches high, and was designed to prevent a freshly buried body being exhumed and sold to the medical men in the city for their anatomy classes.

In 1650 the village was occupied on August 10 by ten companies of Monk's Regiment (now the Coldstream Guards) before they attacked Redhall Castle, then held by Sir James Hamilton. The village also provided a welcome night of rest for the groups of Covenanters trying to escape from Bloody Tam Dalyell's troopers. The Covenanters left Colinton and headed into the Pentlands for their ill-fated stance at Rullion Green while Dalyell's troops crossed the Water at Currie Brig and climbed the long Kirkgate to the hills that way.

There is a suitable monument at Rullion Green to record the battle, and high on the Pentlands there is another poignant reminder of a man who died for his faith. The man fled badly wounded from Rullion Green and headed west towards his Ayrshire home. He was given a night's shelter by Adam Sanders, a farmer, of Blackhill, and food for the next day's journey, but he was too far gone and died. His last wish that he should be buried in sight of his hills of home was carried out; an engraved stone on the Black Law somehow epitomises the strength of character of those who fought so desperately for their beliefs. That stone was placed about 1841, with a suitable service conducted by the minister of nearby Dunsyre.

The ancient Barony of Redhall, which took its name from a house built in red stone, is mentioned in 1292 documents handed by King Edward I to John Balliol and William de Gra(u)nt was its first owner. The barony covered modern Redhall, Oxgangs, Comiston, Swanston, Dreghorn, Bonaly, Woodhall, Colinton and the northern slopes of the Pentlands. When the ancient barony was divided, the lands of Colinton went to John Foulis and by 1540 he had added Swanston, Dreghorn, Baads, Pilmure and Oxgangs to make up the Barony of Colinton – an estate which remained in the family for 350 years. Baads is probably from the Gaelic for a hamlet and was close to Oxgangs, so named after the portion of ground an ox could plough in the course of a year.

Colinton has, of course, developed out of all recognition with booming suburban prosperity, although the old village is centred round the kirk and the quaint street of cottages owned by the Merchant Company. The church itself is full of interest, the 1909 reconstruction work having transformed the 1771 building, which in turn replaced the 1650 structure. An old mort safe stands at the church entrance. It is one of six originally owned and hired out for the protection of newly occupied graves from the resurrectionists.

Among the contents of the graveyard, where Spylaw of Kirkland mill stood from 1585, is the snuff man Gillespie's mausoleum. The stones include a carving for William Niven, weaver in Slateford, which reads 'Death's a dett, to nature due, I have paid it, so must you'.

Colinton manse and its gardens, as mentioned, were familiar places for the young R.L.S. He was fascinated by the sight and sound of the ever-changing water:

> Here is the mill with the humming of thunder,
> Here is the weir with the wonder of foam,
> Here is the sluice with the race running under.
> Marvellous places, though handy to home.

The 'sixpenny tree' at the junction of Colinton Road and Redford Road. After standing for more than 150 years, in 1988 disease was discovered in the branches of the lime, and attempts were made to stop the rot by removing affected branches.

His father was an engineer also connected with the Water of Leith through his plans for the compensation ponds in the Pentlands. One of the young Stevenson's favourite spots was the corner of the wall where the old snuff mill touched the manse grounds.

'The river here is dammed back for the service of the flour mill just below, so that it lies deep and darkling, and the sand slopes into brown obscurity with a glint of gold; and it has been newly recruited by the borrowings of the snuff mill just above, and these tumbling merrily in shake the pool to its black heart, fill it with drowsy eddies, and set the curded froth of many other mills solemnly steering to and fro upon the surface,' writes John Geddie.

Another literary figure connected with the village was Henry Mackenzie who wrote *The Man of Feeling*. He lived in a small thatched cottage at the top of the Bridge Road, and the house is marked with a plaque.

Just about opposite the house is the old 'sixpenny tree', a landmark for the villagers, but under threat from decay. How it got its name is uncertain, but one theory is that local snuff millers would gather there to discuss business and throw sixpenny pieces into a bucket at the foot of the tree for small boys to buy pies.

The area has some of the finest houses in Edinburgh, and among them are properties designed by the distinguished architect Rowand Anderson. Georgian, Victorian, Edwardian, and very modern – they all find a place here.

After passing through the former railway tunnel, the walkway enters one of its most dramatic stretches through the first of the two great gorges of the Water – Colinton Dell. This is a wonderful area of haughland and tumbling stream, wooded and sheltered, but with a charm unequalled on any part of the Water.

The pathway leads down to the village of Slateford, a name mentioned in 1654 when 'James Scobie of Slateford was delated for breaking the Sabbath'. The name comes from the ford which was south of the present road bridge.

Much of the industry which kept the villagers going centres in the working of the Redhall quarries, both now infilled to make public parks, and Hailes quarry. The carting of the stone reached 600 loads a day while the New Town was being built.

The spectacular aqueduct carries the Union Canal over the Water of Leith on its eight arches, a total length of 600 feet. The first passenger boat went into service on the canal in 1822, while the barges carried coal, grain, manure, hides and, of course, stone. The local stage was at Stoneyport, a few hundred yards up the Lanark Road from Slateford. The local stone

The walkway plunges through the old railway tunnel on its way from Colinton to Slateford, and then takes the walker into the spectacular Colinton Dell.

from the Redhall quarries was loaded there.

The arrival of the Edinburgh-Glasgow Railway Company in 1841 foreshadowed the decline of the canal trade, and after the construction of the Slateford viaduct in 1847, the writing was firmly on the wall.

The railway company bought over the canal. The two massive structures, side by side, are a spectacular feat of engineering. Because of its winding nature the Water has many bridges crossing it. When a man called Arrol visited Edinburgh he saw the plans for the new railway line through Colinton and

'The sound of water . . .' such as Robert Louis Stevenson recalled from his boyhood days spent in his grandfather's manse at Colinton. The river gurgles in the beauty of the stretch near Bogsmill.

Currie to Balerno. Although almost bankrupt and though he had never operated on such a scale, he offered to build the rail bridges over the water quickly and cheaply. From there he went on to build bigger bridges – Bothwell, Broomielaw, the second Tay Bridge, the Forth Bridge, London's Tower Bridge. He became Sir William Arrol who died in 1913.

The waters at Slateford claimed the life of one of Currie's ministers who was drowned at 'Sclait fuird' while returning from a meeting of the Edinburgh Presbytery in 1739. 'A serious, honest and worthy pastor, one of the most popular preachers of the time,' read the obituary for the Rev. John Spark in the *Caledonian Mercury*.

In 1886 the village was ravaged by one of the worst outbreaks of cholera the district had known. Its source was thought to be either from cloths brought to the Inglis Green bleachfield, or from rags brought to Kate's Mill. Many people fled the village, shops were closed and the public hall was converted into a temporary hospital.

Beside Slateford Bridge is still the dam which supplied power through a lade to the bleachfield and to a waulk mill. The Inglis Green bleachfield was started in 1773, and was later taken over by George McWhirter, father of the artist John. Still later it became McNab's complex of laundry and dry-cleaning, dyeing and tweedmaking. On the site beside the present Inglis Green Road in the eighteenth century was a grain mill beside which stood Graysmill farmhouse in which Bonnie Prince Charlie spent the night before he and his Highlanders entered the town in 1745.

Slateford and Longstone of all the old villages along the Water have suffered perhaps most from the pressures of modern life – road widening has swept away many old properties, commercial warehouses stretch over the old milling sites in Inglis Green Road, and it's easy to forget the river at this stage in its run.

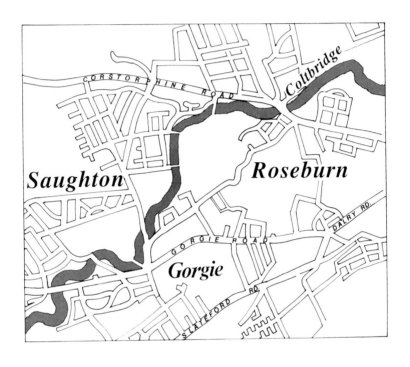

CHAPTER 5

Longstone to Sunbury

Appropriately christened for a village of quarriers, contractors and carters, Longstone got its name from the long stone which crossed the Murrayburn which joins the Water here. Now a footbridge has replaced the stone, and the pathway continues along the perimeter fence of Saughton Prison.

Ahead is the sixteenth-century Stenhouse House built on the lands of Saughton. In 1511 the mill was granted to the Stanhope family, and over the years the name was converted to Stenhouse. It passed to Patrick Ellis, an Edinburgh merchant, who was involved in 'the hame bringing of the strangers from Flanders with their wyffis, bayrins, geir an' work lomes for the makin' of braidclayth and stuffs within the realm'. This was typical of Edinburgh, going to the Continent to find the men able to do the job and furnish training for others, as we have seen in the case of papermaking. When Ellis extended the house in 1623 he had his striking coat of arms and the date placed over the main door. The house is now used as a conservation centre by the Ancient Monuments Division of the Scottish Development Department. During its restoration plaster ceilings were recreated, including one made from the same moulds used in Dalry House in 1661. The house and the nearby cottages seem somewhat misplaced now, surrounded as they are by housing and commercial and industrial development, but they remain a little island in the river's story.

Where Fords Road joins Gorgie Road stands Saughton Bridge, built for the Scottish National Exhibition of 1908 which brought a number of amazing sights for the citizens, including a Senegalese village and a water splash.

The exhibition was in the grounds of the now demolished Saughton House, turned into a spacious public park. Among the current features are the superb rose and scented gardens and the Rose Society's trial ground. The park gates, too, are worth a look, for their ornamental crests. The old house was demolished in a strange way -- because it was riddled with rot Edinburgh Corporation in 1952 agreed it should be burned

Flooding is a problem on some stretches of the Water of Leith and a restoration and repair programme is carried out. Workmen here construct a wall at Roseburn.

down, and a spectacular blaze was organised under the fire service control.

From the dam just upstream from the bridge are visible the remains of the lade gate which took the water to power the Gorgie Mill (with charters in 1236 and 1528) and the wheels at Dalry. Gorgie originally took water from a burn which rose in Craiglockhart, but by 1763 it also had the lade into the Water of Leith.

Gorgie Mill became Cox's Glue Works in 1799 and in 1856 the owner was involved in a battle along with other millowners with the Edinburgh Water Company who had been authorised to undertake the North Pentland Water Scheme. By Act of Parliament the company were empowered to take the water from Colzium Springs and to construct Harperrigg Reservoir which would provide compensation to the Water of Leith. John Cox argued that the water from Harperrigg and from Harlaw Reservoir was of a peaty texture, and did not equal the pure spring water he needed for his business.

NOTICE

Any person annoying or disturbing the swan and wildlife will be prosecuted under the 1981 Country and Wildlife Act

Every notice tells a tale – and at Roseburn a regular nesting place is under observation by nature lovers who give the swans and their family protection.

He told a Parliamentary Committee that before the opening of Harlaw the colour of the glue he produced was 'a medium colour of sherry'. But the glue had become dark when the mossy water from the reservoirs was introduced.

He added: 'The effect was an immense number of complaints as to the quality and colour of my glue. We lost a number of customers and had to submit to a number of deductions and I set my wits to work out how to overcome the evil'.

His concern about the effect on his workers was also apparent – 'They are comfortably housed as labourers in

Only a few hundred yards away from the Water at Roseburn is the Scottish Rugby Union's Murrayfield ground, opened in 1925 with a Calcutta Cup match in which Scotland beat England 14-11. The new stand, seen here, opened in 1983.

Scotland. They have three apartments or two apartments with a large closet. They have a coal yard and a bleaching green and there is a schoolhouse in the village to which a preacher comes on Sunday evening. They have a refreshment place where provisions are sold and also spirituous liquors, but notwithstanding they are an exceedingly well behaved people indeed. I am quite pleased with them and they seem quite happy with me.'

Cox won his case and it was agreed that a supply of spring water should be made available to three mills, the Inglis Green bleachfield and to the Gorgie Glue Works – led by pipes connected with the spring water aqueduct near Clubbiedean and Torduff Reservoirs. The glue works closed in 1969, removing a very distinctive glow from the Gorgie air.

Dalry Mill was part of the site adjacent to Roseburn House which stands near Murrayfield rugby ground, the lade returning to the Water at nearby Coltbridge. As the river passes between Balgreen and Roseburn there is much evidence of attempts to control the flooding to which this stretch is particularly susceptible. Local residents have been pressing councillors for a scheme which will eliminate the danger of flooding entirely.

The Roseburn bridge, erected in 1841 and re-erected in 1930, carries the heavy streams of traffic to and from

The spectacular Donaldson's Hospital which caused the architect Playfair so many problems. Eyed by Queen Victoria as a possible Scottish home, and spoken of as a site for the ill-fated Scottish Assembly, it is a school for deaf youngsters.

Under the arch of Belford Bridge with its distinctive panels of the city arms lies the new housing which now fills the old Sunbury or Coatshaugh distillery site. The bridge was built in 1855-57.

C

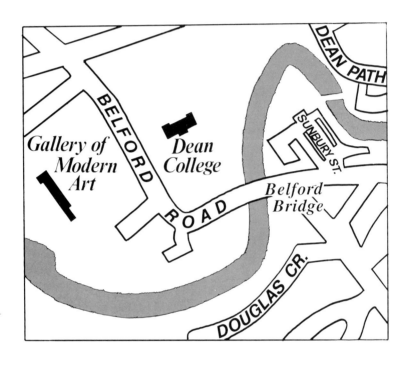

'Gee honey, I sure can hear running water even if we can't see it from the Scottish National Gallery of Modern Art.' The Duane Hanson sculpture 'Tourists' is in the gallery in the former John Watson's Hospital building on the Water's banks at Belford. A stairway down to the riverside from the gallery is being built.

Corstorphine to the West, and just beside it is the old Coltbridge now for pedestrians only.

A piece of bog land between the water and the village of Corstorphine – 'ane aker of land lying bewest the Cowes Bridge (Coltbridge) upon the south side of the little house that stands by the wayside, commonly called the Lamp Aiker' – was an extra emolument for the Corstorphine schoolmaster to ensure that a lantern was hung on the gable of Corstorphine

Kirk to guide travellers across the bog. Indeed, the bog was so wet that provisions could be taken by shallow boat from Coltbridge to Corstorphine.

It was at Coltbridge that the famous (or infamous) 'Coltbridge Canter' was enacted in 1745. A group of the 13th and 14th Dragoons of Sir John Cope's cavalry were driven into inglorious rout simply by seeing a batch of Prince Charlie's Highlanders rushing at them. Legend has it that the dragoons raced to Drumsheugh and didn't stop till they reached Leith.

The old Lochrin Burn, in parts a notorious open sewer which drained the Meadows, joined the Water at Coltbridge. Nowadays the waterside is very pleasing, with houses and their gardens right down to the edge, as the river approaches classical Edinburgh.

The broad haugh below the former John Watson's College, now the National Gallery of Modern Art, is a swathe of open ground still, despite developments on the high banks above. Donaldson's Hospital, another of the endowments of a thankful and successful businessman, was designed by William Playfair between 1841 and 1851. The sum of £210,000 was left by James Donaldson, the proprietor of the *Edinburgh Gazette*, an enterprising newspaperman.

During the Napoleonic War, as a morale as well as circulation booster, he instructed his printers to add 0's to the figures of French killed in battle – so much so that it was calculated at the end of the war that Donaldson had killed off more than the entire population of that country.

There was great consideration before the final design for his hospital, now a school for deaf youngsters, was accepted by the trustees. Leading architects of the day were asked to compete. Work eventually started in 1842, twelve years after Donaldson's death, and finished in 1851 – 'that eternal Donaldson's Hospital,' said Playfair. The sweep of the river takes it past the Hilton Hotel, the granary building a reminder of Bell's Mill which stood on the site used for milling since the 1100s. The last mill was destroyed in an explosion in 1975.

The Belford Bridge, under which the walkway goes, was originally built in 1784 to carry the old Queensferry Road which went through the Water of Leith Village (now Dean). The renewed bridge of 1855-57 carries superb city and royal

A world apart – a study of anglers at peace with the world on the walkway at the Hilton National Hotel which was built (as the Dragonara) on the site of Bell's Mill.

crests clearly visible on both sides of the ramparts. Now we are into Sunbury, occupied by town houses and flats on the ground originally called Coatshaugh and at one time the site of a large distillery, Haig's.

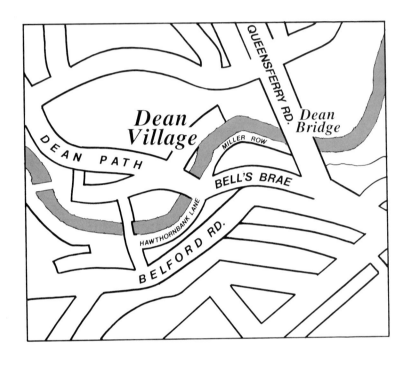

CHAPTER 6
The Dean Valley

Of the Water of Leith villages, the Dean Village, as we now call it, is the most easily identifiable as a community, nowadays indeed a growing community, and still self-contained. 'The mylnes of Dene' were listed, as we have seen, in the King David I charter, proving the antiquity of the buildings which originally stood in this very attractive part of the city. Now the village is readily seen from the Dean Bridge and the shape of the expansions with new housing contrasting with the older buildings is very apparent. And when you hear that a penthouse flat reached a price of £237,000 in the spring of 1988, you realise just how attractive it can be.

The original village of Dean stood close to the site of the Dean Cemetery on the slopes to the north of the milling hamlet then called the Water of Leith. Close by was the old mansion house of Dean, demolished in 1845 to make way for the cemetery which contains some of the most fascinating funeral sculptures of any in the city and is the last resting place of many influential citizens. The remnants of the old village of Dean were cleared in the early 1880s.

Down by the waterside, the Baxters Incorporation of Edinburgh held sway in the milling lands – this body controlled the rights to grinding their own grain and generally looking after their own interests before anything else.

There is ample evidence of their presence in the carved stones of the baking trade of the Baxters, and over the years the mills have come and gone. There is a reference in Town Council minutes in the sixteenth century to 'eleven common mylnes upon bath the sydis of the Water of Leith'.

The sense of milling is still apparent with the dams at the Sunbury end of the village, and just downstream from the bridge crossing the Water by the huge West Mill, now converted into flats. At the foot of Bell's Brae is the Baxters' Tolbooth, a 1675 building that was used as the Incorporation headquarters and as a granary. The carving on its side shows the bakers' crossed peels, three cakes and a pie and the

Reflections in a river. More and more modern housing is springing up in the Dean Village as the popularity of waterside living is appreciated by developers and homebuyers.

inscription reads: 'God's Providence is our Inheritance' and 'God bless the Baxters of Edinburgh who built this Hous 1675'. Just across the cobbled street, on the wall beside the bridge parapet are two more carved stones which came from Lindsay's Mill, a datestone 1643, also with crossed peels, and a lintel bearing the words 'Blessit be God for all His Giftis'.

The site of Lindsay's Mill, the outline of which can still be seen, is marked by grinding wheels and a 'sitooterie' on Miller Row, the start of the riverside walk to Stockbridge. Architects' offices, which have blended in well with the older part of the village, stand on the site of the famous 'Jericho' granary built in 1619. It was destroyed by fire in the 1950s.

Across the village bridge and behind the school building, also converted to housing, stands Well Court, a square of red

Laid out by Edinburgh architect David Cousin on the grounds of Dean House, the Dean Cemetery contains spectacular statuary. Side by side on this west wall lie four of the city's most distinguished men of last century – Lord (Francis) Jeffrey, lawyer and man of letters; Lord (Andrew) Rutherford, the conveyancer; the architect William Playfair; and Lord (Henry) Cockburn, judge, advocate and Edinburgh preservationist.

sandstone buildings which were financed by John Ritchie Findlay, proprietor of *The Scotsman*. The clock-tower building was designed as a community hall, but is now used as an office.

A lively Village Association have kept an anxious eye on planning applications which have threatened to spoil the village uniqueness.

To relieve the hard work of their daily existence, the Baxters had gala days, or gaudé-days, and the most eagerly anticipated was the annual outing to the village mills at the 'Feeing of the Millers'. Alison Hay Dunlop describes such an event in 1716: 'In the fair spring weather of the same year of grace the Deacon and remanent members of their special trade-council left the town behind. We almost think we see them – douce, staid, vigorous old and elderly men in wigs, square-cut coats, long vests, knee-breeches and three-cornered hats.

The Dean Village in 1965 – picturesque but showing signs of neglect. The old school building in the centre and the building on the right have since been renovated for housing. On the left is Well Court.

> They gang by twa, they gang by thrie,
> Oot ower the bent sae broon,
> And the neibours look frae ilk stair-head
> As they step wast the toun.

'Yes, 'step' is the word, not 'walk'; neither do they talk at this early stage of the day's proceedings – they rotate, just a little; but their speech will grow more natural, not to say flowing, as the hours of that day roll on. On every face there is that indescribable look of grave wisdom and 'wecht' which is inseparable, even when on pleasure bent, from the earliest stage of official life, deepened as it is in the present instance by conscious incorporation prosperity.'

'There is also that difference of height and figure in sharp contrast and in close arm-and-arm conjunction, which appears to be another standing feature of incorporated existence. It is Baxterdom of 'the auncient royalty' – of Edinburgh within its

The closeness of the community in the old Water of Leith Village is readily seen. The former Holy Trinity Church at the northern end of the Dean Bridge was used as an electricity sub-station, but has now reverted to ecclesiastical use.

walls, that is represented, the Canongate being 'thirled' to its own Canon-mills.'

'They pass through the Grassmarket out by the West Port into Portsburgh, which in its own place and degree has also its tale of craft Incorporations. With them it is not a gaudé-day; but they also come to their outside stairheads, and lean over their half shop-doors, and gaze after the review of the brethren from the very adjacent city.'

'Arrived at the mills, and having transacted their business, and settled generally and specifically as to what moiety of wages should be in money and what in meal – and we have the authority of an ancient miller that these engagements were better than under a single master, the Incorporation being furthy and rowthy and no at a' scrimpit – the Deacons and the council adjourned to the hostelry of William Gordon to dine. The dinner is marked alike by simplicity and substantiality.'

The stone is wearing with the passage of time, but the Baxters'
symbols are still visible on the old granary building in the Dean Village
– a wheatsheaf, cherubs' heads, two crossed peels with a pie and three
cakes and a pair of scales. The lettering reads: GOD BLESS THE
BAXTERS OF EDINBRUGH WHO BUILT THIS HOUS 1675.

'The meal account is detailed in full - 'Beef and veall, and
broth and breid,' followed in due course by 'pypes and
tobacko'. The liquors are – not whisky, but 'brandie and eal'. A
course of free trade, of which tales might be told, existed
between the kingdom of France and sundry villages on the
Water of Leith, in the matter of brandy and claret, long before
the time of Cobden and the Commercial Treaty, and a strong
heavy ale, that is described as gluing the lips together while
drinking, was in favour by both gritters and millers, only there
is good reason to suspect that the cohesion would be of but a
temporary nature.'

And so a happy day was had by all, because the account
related that the guildsmen 'did not forget the small and the
millworkers too enjoyed the feast day'.

Miss Dunlop relates that the millers of the Water of Leith
were 'massive men – famed as such at Calder Fair, even
amongst the tall men of the Lothians'. Writing in 1890, she

Reminders of an earlier day. The Dean Village Association fayre and pageant in 1987 brought out these ladies in period costume for the event. The Association still keep a close eye on development plans for the village.

adds: 'Our early remembrance of them is as a series of human hillsides powdered white – and their hands – were there ever such comfortably large hands! A gowpenfull of groats from the good-natured giant who kept the oat-kiln, and whose doorstep and barn-door were ever covered by a perennial yet constantly shifting population of eident sparrows, was largesse in magnitude! . . .'

'But to our Baxters, as to other people, feast-day and fast-day fare to an end. With their three-cornered hats just a thought awry, and their Sunday kirk-wigs a trifle agee, they climb up the steep Bell's Brae, now spanned by the Dean Bridge; they turn in the still clear evening light, not to view the far Firth with its softened shores and its sleeping islands, but each and all pause and look down for a parting glance on their property and their prosperity, their great granary, with its legend – 'God Bliss the Baxters o' Edinburgh who Built this Hous' – their people with the certainty of work and the sureness of bread

The water roars over the dam at the West Mill, now converted into flats. There was a mill on the site from at least the mid-sixteenth century, and the present building is early nineteenth century.

before them, then turning their faces comfortably citywards, past Meldrumsheughe, past the West Kirk, past the now darkening Castle rock – to quote the overword of one of their own old songs – they gang toddlin' hame:

> As round as a neep,
> Or as lang as a leek,
> They gang toddlin' hame.

In addition to those who found work in the mills, agricultural labourers on the nearby farms and carter quarrymen at Craigleith, where much of the stone which built the New Town was hewn, lived in the village which in the eighteenth century consisted of a single short street with two or three lanes heading off.

Cumberland Hill, an authority on this stretch of the water, says that in 1743 the population of the Dean, according to a census presented to the ministers of St Cuthbert's Parish Church (the West Kirk) was: Families 85; men 107, women 157, boys 68, girls 63. Total number of males 175. Total number of females 220. Total number of the population 395.

It is worth noting that Abercrombie and Plumstead describe the then Dean as 'rather a confused conglomeration of buildings which derive a considerable amount of charm in certain instances from such irregularity. In fact anything but an informal layout for such a development in such a deep ravine as here would be absurd'. Forty years on, look from the Dean Bridge onto the village and there is in fact a frightening formality about some of the new layouts.

After the flour mills, the other major work in the village was weaving. The Incorporation of Weavers of the Water of Leith had a 'seal of cause' granted by the Baron Bailie of Broughton in 1728, but by the latter half of the nineteenth century that trade had vanished. Cumberland Hill in 1887 relates: 'We remember the long range of weaving shops by the dam side, and also at the back of the West Mill. The merry clack of the shuttle was heard the live long day; winding pirns was an employment for the old women, and many of the boys of the village were employed as draw boys – that is boys who helped the weaver to draw through the long warp threads in the loom. Some beautiful work was wont to be produced here; not only in linen and damask, but also in 'filled in shawls' – a manufacture now transferred to Paisley'.

A branch of the Friends of the People was founded in the village after the French Revolution had sparked off in Britain a demand for Parliamentary reform, and the more ardent members were prepared to use force to achieve their aims if necessary. Two of the most active members were Robert Orrock, the blacksmith up the hill at Dean, and one of the weavers, Arthur McEwan. Orrock hammered out on his forge some pikes and a Lochaber axe, ready for the call to arms. But they appeared to have second thoughts and as members of the Water of Leith Society of the Friends of the People and members of the British Convention were witnesses for the Crown against other members of the convention, including Robert Watt and David Downie, a city wine merchant and goldsmith respectively.

The two men were found guilty and sentenced to die on October 15, 1794. Downie was subsequently spared. The government's determination to stamp out the radical

The majestic Dean Bridge which is one of Thomas Telford's greatest
engineering feats. Nowadays it is a primary traffic route to the city
centre. The parapets had to be raised to prevent potential suicides
throwing themselves into the river.

movement obviously frightened some members of the Water of
Leith Society and all the pikes were said to have been thrown
into the river. Some were found later when a major drainage
scheme was carried out last century.

The most spectacular of all the bridges which span the Water
is unquestionably the Dean Bridge, carrying thousands of
vehicles daily on a main city centre traffic artery. It has been
carrying traffic since 1831, and its design and construction by
Thomas Telford is recognised as one of his best, and most
enduring, engineering feats. The four-arched bridge is 106
feet above the water surface and was the idea of Lord Provost

Sir John Learmonth who wanted to open up his estate of Dean for housebuilding as part of the New Town expansion. But the gorge of the Water of Leith at this point was a major stumbling block.

Encouraged by the success of the Earl of Moray in his feuing of sites on his estate on the southern side of the river, Learmonth appointed Telford to tackle the task of bridging the river. It is said that the wood scaffolding erected as the stone pillars and arches were constructed was in itself a great work of art. Cumberland Hill recalls that the start of the work in the morning was regulated by the practice of 'beating the mett'. This was an ancient custom connected with the mills, and one of the millers beat a large corn measure (or mett) with a rolling pin and the sound carried up and down the valley. As the echoes rolled round the gorge the gangers set to, and the structure rose steadily. When the stonework was completed the job of removing the scaffolding had to be strictly overseen to allow an equal settlement of the Craigleith stone over the length of the bridge. Its total length is 447 feet and it is 39 feet broad, linking the dramatic drop at Randolph Cliff with the former Trinity Episcopal Church, built in 1838 to a design by John Henderson, at the northern end. This building for many years housed an electricity sub-station, and is now reverting to ecclesiastical use.

For Lord Provost Learmonth, however, the project was a bit of a disaster initially; the boom in housebuilding dried up and it was a further twenty years before the Dean feus were taken up and work started on the building of Clarendon Crescent.

The Dean Bridge is now one of the best known in the city. Because of its height it has attracted a fair number of suicides over the years. The problem had reached such proportions that in 1888 the Burgh Engineer John Cooper was asked to report on ways of preventing people leaping from the then low parapet to their death in the water below. Among his suggestions was studding the parapet cope with barbed spikes – 'somewhat unsightly and might on a windy day prove troublesome'. He thought a system of spiked bars, curved upwards and inwards on the outward side of the bridge, 'of sufficiently threatening aspect to deter anyone attempting to leap . . .' He added, however: 'Considerable sensation might be

Inside the Dean Bridge. While the traffic rumbles overhead, an engineer carries out the regular inspection of the four arches of the bridge, built between 1829-31.

caused to the neighbourhood by anyone dropping down upon it and requiring to be rescued'. At the end of the day the parapet was raised to a uniform height, with the 'least possible injury' which Mr Cooper wanted to inflict on the bridge.

If you look over the bridge at the Randolph Cliff end you can see in the corner of a garden a small statue of a young man looking across to the bridge itself. One apocryphal story says it was erected in memory of a sailor who wanted to impress his lady love and jumped from the parapet using an umbrella to slow his successful descent. He did it twice without injury, but tempting fate, he tried again and met the inevitable end.

Another tale has it that the man jumped for a bet. It has been suggested that such stories of derring-do deserved a statue, but more mundanely the figure appears to have been simply a piece of garden statuary ordered by the then proprietor of the house and executed by a sculptor in his studio in Poorhouse Lane near the West End.

In his 'poem on that beautiful scene between the Dean Bridge and Saint Bernard's Mineral Well on the Water of Leith at Edinburgh', Robert McCandless commented:

> There I next espy'd,
> In a garden all alone,
> A man who sat,
> and out of that,
> To move he was never known.
> For, night or day,
> Should you pass that way,
> You'll find him sitting there;
> Weather, cold or hot,
> That's his spot,
> And a solid stone's his chair.

We pass beneath the Dean Bridge along the walkway and past the remains of Greenland Mill at the base of the gardens of Randolph Cliff and Crescent and the ornamental gardens of the Moray Estate. The great slabs of those buildings have moved several commentators to point out that the houses were built the wrong way round – their backs overlook the valley and a wonderful opportunity was lost to make them the most dramatic town houses in Edinburgh by having the crescents face the water.

That doughty defender of the city against the planning vandals of his day, the judge Lord Cockburn, was one who felt that way – 'everything sacrificed to the multiplicity of feuing feet'. He was equally pertinent about the plan for the New Town generally, it must be added: '. . . we were led into the blunder of long straight lines of streets, divided to an inch, and all to the same number of inches, by rectangular intersections, every house being an exact duplicate of its neighbour, with a

dexterous avoidance, as if from horror, of every ornament or
excrescence by which the slightest break might vary the
surface. What a site did nature give us for our New Town! Yet
what insignificance in its plan! What poverty in all its details!'

The ornamental gardens are a feature of this part of the
Water with the Dean Gardens on the opposite bank and
Belgrave Gardens just upstream from the Dean Bridge. The
kitchen gardens, old buildings and general clutter between the
select Belgrave Crescent and the Dean Village was cleared in
1876 and Belgrave Gardens were created. Somewhat earlier
residents who had finally moved into Clarendon Crescent, Eton
Terrace and the other developing streets at the northern end
of the bridge were alarmed in 1867 at suggestions that Lord
Provost Learmonth's son was thinking of constructing another
street of houses, to be called Cambridge Terrace, on the site
opposite Eton Terrace. With some reluctance Colonel
Learmonth finally agreed that a pleasure garden could be laid
out instead, and the Trustees of Sir Henry Raeburn gave
ground at the end of Ann Street to add to the gardens.

For about £400 gardens were laid out, but because
Learmonth was still keen to build more houses, the committee
of feuars were faced with the prospect of either buying the
ground for themselves or seeing all their good work going to
waste and the unwanted houses being constructed. Thankfully
for future generations a levy was raised and in 1876 the lands
of what are now the Dean Gardens were bought for more than
£2500. Users continue to pay an annual fee for a garden key,
and have to meet the cost of maintenance.

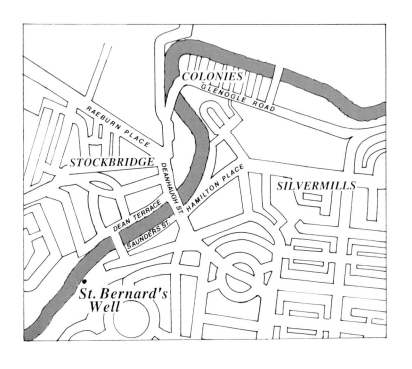

CHAPTER 7

Stockbridge and Silvermills

A mill lade ran on wooden supports on the southern bank of the Water of Leith to feed Silvermills and Canonmills, but the best-known feature now at this stretch is probably St Bernard's Well. The healing powers of the mineral waters from the well were brought to the public's attention by a notice in the *Scots Magazine* in 1760: 'A mineral well has lately been discovered between the village and the Water of Leith and Stockbridge, about half a mile north of Edinburgh, which is said to be equal in quality to any of the most famous in Britain. To preserve the well from the injury of the weather, and prevent its being overflowed by the Water of Leith, on the banks of which it is situated, a stone covering is to be erected over it. The foundation-stone of this building was laid September 15th (by a deputation from the Earl of Leven, the present Grand Master of Scotland), by Alexander Drummond, brother of Provost Drummond, lately British Consul at Aleppo, and Provincial Grand Master of all the Lodges in Asia and in Europe, out of Britain, holding of the Grand Lodge of Scotland. He was attended by many brethren in their proper clothing and insignia, preceded by a band of music, and the ceremony was performed in the presence of a great number of spectators. It is called St Bernard's Well'.

What the original structure was like is uncertain, but the well rapidly grew in popularity – the mineral water comes from a source separate from the Water of Leith and was in fact available until 1956 when an investigation by public health analysts found that 'the possibility of the well water being contaminated could not be ruled out'.

The well in the early days gave Stockbridge the reputation of a spa, and it was purchased in August 1788 by one of the great characters of the day. Lord Gardenstone, the judge, was an ardent believer in the well's efficacy, and he set about getting a suitable covering for it. The inspiration for the design by Alexander Naysmith of the dome-topped building was taken from the temple at Tivoli in Italy, and a statue of the goddess of health Hygeia was incorporated. Initially free from vandalism, she has suffered badly in recent years, her arms having been damaged and her body daubed.

His Lordship laid down instructions for the use of his well, including the furnishing of 'proper glasses and cups'. George Murdoch, the Stockbridge man appointed by the judge as its first keeper, was told to charge 'grown persons' one penny and children one halfpenny for a glass of water during the morning period; at other times free access could be had. And Lord Gardenstone also laid down a proper procedure for sampling the waters: 'The proper and customary method of drinking at mineral waters is, that persons after drinking a glass or cup retire immediately and walk about, or take other exercise for an interval of at least five minutes, both as a benefit to themselves, and to make way for other water drinkers. A contrary practice prevails at St Bernard's, and sometimes a crowd of people continue at the well till they have drunk their quota. Hereafter every person must retire as above, and the keeper must require them to do so, this regulation being very necessary'.

Lord Gardenstone, formerly Francis Garden, was a very distinguished lawyer, being raised to the bench in 1764. He is said to have been one of those worthies who in his early days as an advocate could spend the night carousing and then plead most eloquently in court next morning, without having had a sleep or even, on occasion, without having read his papers.

Among his eccentricities was a great love of pigs; he had raised one as a pet, much as another man would treat a dog. As a piglet he allowed it to crawl into bed beside him – although when it grew to full size it had to be content with a couch in his master's room where it warmed the judge's clothing. He also consumed vast quantities of snuff, having a special leather pocket round his waistcoat to carry copious quantities.

When he signed the feu charter for St Bernard's Well, Lord Gardenstone agreed to entertain the superiors yearly with four magnum bottles of the most excellent claret. The mineral waters must have been beneficial, or maybe it was the claret and snuff, for his Lordship died peacefully in his Morningside house in 1793 at the age of 71.

The Well in due course passed to Mr William Nelson, of the

distinguished Edinburgh printing firm. He restored the building, including the mosaic and marble interior, and had a new approach built with a broad stair from St Bernard's Bridge. On completion of the work he passed the well into the care of the Town Council.

Just upstream is the site of another mineral well, which was used briefly – the little stone building over St George's Well. Because of its closeness to the wells, the street we now call Upper Dean Terrace was, when first built, named Mineral Street. It stands at the end of one of the most attractive and sought-after (judging by the six-figure sums now asked for the house) little throughfares in the city, Ann Street. This was built on land owned by the painter Sir Henry Raeburn whose St Bernard's House and lands were on that side of the river. He married a widow, Ann Leslie of Deanhaugh. Ann Street was started in 1817 and its great charm lies in the front gardens which stretch to the narrow roadway from the elegant houses. With so much of the New Town and its extensions plain-fronted with shared ornamental gardens, the houses on Raeburn's estate are a reminder of how attractive such individual gardens are. Even in the busy Raeburn Place where shops have supplanted gardens in front of the original houses, you can still see one or two gardens, while there are plots of greenery also in Dean Street.

When it came to feuing his property as part of the housing boom, Sir Henry, who was born in Stockbridge in 1756, was anxious to lay down strict controls for the properties in St Bernard's Crescent, Danube Street (designated Charlotte Street), Carlton Street, Dean Terrace and the unfeued lots in Ann Street. He stipulated that none of the houses should be occupied as shops or taverns, although the back parts of the houses in St Bernard's Crescent might be used for such purposes, with a Dean Street entry. He set down limits for the number of flats in a common stair, and wanted the balconies to

---

Slightly battered and showing signs of vandalism, St Bernard's Well is still a most attractive site near Stockbridge. Following a successful trial in 1988, the well-house may be opened to the public on a regular basis.

New Town Councillor David Guest, who was instrumental in winning public access to the well-house, stands under the mosaic dome beside the old pump. The building was erected by Lord Gardenstone, who purchased the mineral well in 1788.

be of the same pattern as No 57 West Northumberland Street, while railings were to follow the design of those in West Heriot Row.

The bustle of building on the banks beside Stockbridge evoked the following regrets from Robert Chambers, the historian and author, in his *Walks in Edinburgh* in 1825: 'Still

Lord Gardenstone – in his time a stalwart of the Scottish bar and bench – is captured in this sketch by Kay. But he will be best remembered for his eccentricities, including keeping a pig as a pet and allowing it to sleep in his room.

farther to the west lies Stockbridge, which gives name to a sort of village, now surrounded, and partly destroyed, by the encroaching limits of the rapidly-extending city. The glen here formed by the Water of Leith was, till lately, a beautifully and sequestered natural scene; but its echoes, which formerly answered only to the melody of birds and the fall of waters, are now disturbed by the rude sound of the mechanic's hammer and almost destroyed outright by the alterations in the character of the ground'.

Well, whatever he thought, few would disagree that the majority of the building on Raeburn's former grounds reached a high standard. On the site of Ann Street for a while stood a curious block of stone once intended to be sculpted into a statue of Oliver Cromwell. After the block had been landed at Leith, the Town Council heard of the Protector's death, so the act of obsequiousness became an unnecessary expense. The block – the statue was planned for Parliament Close off the

Ann Street – one of THE streets in Edinburgh's New Town and one of the few where each house has a front garden. Named by Sir Henry Raeburn, its developer, in memory of his wife.

High Street – lay neglected on Leith Sands until in 1778 Walter Ross, a Writer to the Signet and Registrar of Distillery Licences in Scotland, had it placed on the rising ground he held above the Water of Leith. The stone had been roughly prepared and looked like a giant trunk with stumps of arms. After Ross died, it lay neglected, but about 1825 it was briefly erected on a pedestal on a vacant site in Ann Street before being broken up.

Ross, who was known for his enthusiasm for the arts as well as his sense of humour, had a tower, known locally as 'Ross's folly', on his land. It resembled a Border peel (keep) house and stood about forty feet high with a room on ground and upper level. After he had finished laying out his pleasure gardens round the tower, Ross found he was being plagued by vandals. He warned that spring guns and man traps were set to threaten intruders, but to no avail. So he came up with a scheme, matching his reputation for humour with a quiet determination to protect his property. He acquired a human leg from the Royal Infirmary, had it decorated with a stocking and shoe, and had the town crier show it off.

The crier announced that the leg had been found the previous night in Mr Ross's Stockbridge grounds, and said it

Sir Henry Raeburn, the portrait painter, who was born in Stockbridge in 1756, lived in St Bernard's House after his marriage to Ann Leslie of Deanhaugh. He laid down strict conditions for the building of houses in what are now St Bernard's Crescent, Danube Street, Carlton Street, Dean Terrace and Ann Street. National Galleries of Scotland photo.

would readily be returned to the owner if he came forward. The point was made, and Mr Ross could enjoy his summer house in peace.

Raeburn was not the only distinguished artist to know Stockbridge well. In Church Lane – the route taken by parishioners heading up the hill to St Cuthbert's Church – stands Duncan's Land, where David Roberts was born in 1796. The house is often mistakenly assumed to be much older than it is because the lintel over the door carries the inscription 'Fear God Onlye 1605. I.R.' The stone was taken from the house demolished in the Lawnmarket when Bank Street was being driven through at the top of the Mound. Church Lane has been renamed Gloucester Street, thus pointlessly removing a little local touch from the area.

Another distinguished Edinburgh artist, David Roberts, was born in
Duncan's Land, in the original Church Lane at Stockbridge, The 1605
lintel stone came from a building demolished in Edinburgh's
Lawnmarket, and the house itself is late eighteenth-century.

Another artist with Stockbridge connections was Robert Scott
Lauder who was born in the hamlet of Silvermills in 1803 and
lived for some years before his death in 1869 in Carlton Street.

Cumberland Hill says that about 1826 there was a 'Six Foot
Club' in Stockbridge for athletes who reached that height.
They practised on a small park at the back of Malta Terrace,
generally in the morning, and then breakfasted together before
going to their jobs, mainly in banks and public offices. These
men would certainly have been familiar with the old mill lade
which ran past the two mineral wells and along Saunders
Street to carry water to Silvermills and Canonmills, further
evidence of how the Water's use could be stretched far from its
bed to provide power for many purposes. The development
northwards and westwards of the New Town meant that the

Stockaree – the bustling centre through which the Water passes. The distinctive tower of the former Stockbridge Free Church is now incorporated into sheltered housing, while another landmark is the Trustee Savings Bank with its clock tower.

city was faced with a huge sewage disposal problem, and less scrupulous builders were quite happy to use the Water of Leith as a dumping ground for all sorts of refuse, including human sewage.

Dr Henry Littlejohn, Edinburgh's first and great pioneering Medical Officer of Health, who lived in Royal Circus just above Stockbridge Village, prepared in 1865 a very detailed *Report on Sanitary Conditions*. He states that the Water of Leith not only drained 'the whole of the New Town north of George Street, but also received the sewage of a large district of the city lying to the west which joins at Coltbridge . . . At present the Water of Leith, in its passage through Edinburgh, is a great open sewer, subject to considerable fluctuations in the volume of its waters; and in hot weather, during the prevalence of certain winds, it emits offensive odours'.

Dr Littlejohn said that especially since the formation of the Caledonian Distillery, 'most unfortunately situated' (at Haymarket), the smell had been much complained of, as it was impossible to pass the refuse from such a large establishment into any of the sewers. 'All the strongly offensive material was discharged into the Lochrin Burn, an open drain running westward, and conveying a large amount of sewage into the Water of Leith, which in its turn entered the city and passed through the village of the Water of Leith, Stockbridge, and Canonmills, on its way to the sea. The inhabitants were thus subjected to a double annoyance. During westerly winds, the odour of the refuse before it reached Coltbridge was carried over the town, and in its further progress infested all the districts along both banks of the Water of Leith. What added to the nuisance was a great diminution effected in the Water of Leith itself by the supply granted to mills along its course'.

'In summer these mill-lades left the main stream dry, and conveyed not pure water, but sewage through densely-peopled localities.'

Despite all this, however, Dr Littlejohn found to his surprise that the district was generally a healthy one – 'The population was clustered along the banks of a stream proved by analysis to be fraught with the most noxious compounds; and were the views commonly held by sanitary reformers correct, we should not only have had the presence of this pestiferous stream

D

Beside the Savings Bank, built about 1840 with the clock tower added in 1900, another sign to show the way to the walkway to the Colonies – an intriguing part of Edinburgh's history: a nineteenth-century co-operative building development.

indicated by a largely increased death-rate, but also by a mortality depending upon the presence of such diseases as fevers, diarrhoea, and dysentery . . .'

The death rates of the Upper and Lower Water of Leith districts for 1863 were respectively 19 and 17 per 1000 – 'when we remember the large number of inhabitants in these districts belonging to the working-class, and also that since the census of 1861 the population has been increased by the addition of several new streets, these figures must be regarded as highly satisfactory'.

He also outlined just what living conditions on the banks of the Water were like: 'One locality in the district of the Upper Water of Leith presents a very dense population, and has a correspondingly high mortality. I refer to that triangular area bounded by India Place, Saunders Street and Kerr Street. One of the sides is bounded by the stream of the Water of Leith, while it is intersected by an open mill lade, notorious for its impurities. The distance of the nearest houses in this locality from the Water of Leith is only 12 yards, while that of the most distant is 93 yards. Here the inhabitants are densely crowded in the proportion of 516.7 to the acre, the death rate is 26.86, while that of children under 5 rises to 106.67. But on examining the nature of the mortality, we find such diseases as are the product of a dense population, and not those generally attributed to sewage exhalations'.

'To the north we have another densely-peopled district, of a triangular shape, bounded by Dean Street on the one hand, and Mary Place on the other, and containing such streets as Allan Street, Cheyne Street, Bedford Street and Hermitage Street. The nearest point of this district to the Water of Leith is 120 yards, and the most distant 283 yards. The density of the population is, however, considerably less, being only 366.9 to the acre, and the total death-rate is 25.02, while that of children under 5 years is as high as 69.07.'

'But here again, we fail to find any indication in the nature of the mortality that the high death-rate is due to any other cause than overcrowding.'

'In the district of the Lower Water of Leith, at only one point, viz, at Canonmills, have we a poor population collected in any number. The death-rate for 1863 is 24.88, while that of children above 5 years is 108.34. There, however, we have a large poor population, and, in many circumstances, wretchedly housed.'

The Upper Water of Leith, however, showed a 'very marked mortality' from diphtheria: 'the measure for the purification of the Water of Leith must be looked upon as an important sanitary measure to be followed, at no late period, it is to be hoped, by the removal or improvement of the mills, which at present divert the run of the water, leaving a channel of the stream for the most part dry, and which are a source of nuisance, besides necessitating the continued preservation of the mill lades. The latter were perfectly innocuous when the district was purely a rural one and some miles from the city but they are now quite an anomaly in the midst of a large population, and ought, sooner or later, to be removed'.

Dr Littlejohn's district of the Upper Water of Leith included Donaldson's and John Watson's Hospitals and the (Dean) Orphan Hospital, the old village of the Water of Leith and 'the

New sheltered housing
towers over a solitary
fisherman on the stretch
between Stockbridge
and Falshaw Bridge.
The branches on the left
hang from trees in the
gardens of Saxe-Coburg
Place houses.

modern suburb of Stockbridge'. The Lower area was 'mainly a
rural district, with a limited population, chiefly confined to the
southern bank of the stream. It contains the remains of the
ancient village of Canonmills, in which many of the houses still
preserve the wretched character of the poorer class of country
dwellings of the last century'.

He reminded the city councillors in his report that there was
a cholera epidemic in Edinburgh in 1848 and fever epidemics
in 1847-8 and 1857-8. In the two districts he noted the following
manufactories and trades: breweries 1; tanneries 4; flour mills
5; dye works 2; chemical works 1; builders 2; cat-gut
manufacturer 1.

The Town Council and Commissioners of Police produced a
report in 1853 on the condition of the Water between St
Bernard's Well and Warriston Cemetery, and suggested
various improvements including the laying of continuous pipes
and conduits at an estimated cost of £5000. This was a start,
and in 1864 an Act was presented to provide main and branch

sewers and works from Coltbridge right down the river to Easter Craigs on the Black Rock at Leith Sands. The Act also made it an offence to discharge refuse into the river above Coltbridge. Sweeping changes involving alterations to mill lades, cauls and dams in the stretch from Coltbridge as far down the river as Bonnington were made in further major sanitary improvements by an Act before the 1886 session of Parliament.

Gradually the use of the Water of Leith as an open sewer was curtailed with the introduction of piping, and the pollution latterly was primarily from mills pouring untreated effluent into the stream.

It is easily forgotten that in what is now almost entirely an urban area, there were countless farms with their byres, and many a villager or miller would have a cow shed. A report in *The Builder* of February 16, 1867, commenting on the sanitary conditions of the New Town, relates: 'One other nuisance is the condition of the many byres which exist in the New Town, or rather the old out-houses or stables, which are used as such. Between 800 and 900 cows are housed in these, or, at least, were immediately prior to the outbreak of the rinderpest'. The report adds: 'One decided discomfort, if not of disease, prevails to a great extent, and even in some of the most fashionable streets. On the wall of the butchers' and fleshers' shops, which are ordinarily placed in the most prominent positions at the street corners, may be seen exposed the carcasses of oxen, sheep and pigs, together with their skins and offal. These are not only eyesores, destroying the amenity of the neighbourhood, but they taint the surrounding atmosphere with a strong effluvium'.

Stockbridge was long outside the old town, a pleasant place for a long walk, or perhaps a weekend in the country, and the mineral waters unquestionably increased its attractiveness. One derivation of the name is from the original wooden, or stock, footbridge across the stream which saved pedestrians the trouble of fording. And for the carters the ford does seem to have caused some problems with a steep incline into the water from both banks. When the water was high the carters had to manhandle their goods across the little bridge. In due course a proper stone bridge was built in 1786 and then the present one

Quiet beauty in the middle of a busy city. The Water of Leith winds round the haugh where the Colonies were built to provide homes mostly for artisan subscribers. A particular feature is the outside stair leading to the upper houses.

was constructed in 1901-2.

The village fell within the parish of St Cuthbert's; two of the ministers, the Rev. Neil McVicar and the Rev. Thomas Pitcairn, carried out a census in 1743 which listed a total population of the village at 524 – 156 men, 188 women, 105 boys and 75 girls – all in 120 families. Many of the population would have found work with the flour mills and tan pits, and about 1814 a china pottery was started at Dean Bank, near where Saxe-Coburg Place stands. Some pieces of Stockbridge china are in the city museum, but the work was short-lived.

We have already heard from Dr Littlejohn that living conditions in the middle of last century were not too comfortable for many of the villagers – in his 1865 report he notes incidentally there were 107 millers in the city, 400 tanners, 225 tobacco and snuff manufacturers. For the womenfolk the choice was much more restricted – 13,949 were domestic servants, and few New Town houses would have been

able to operate without the servants ranging from the scullery lass to the mistress's maid; while 5388 found a living as milliner, dressmaker or seamstress.

Something of the depressing nature of life in nineteenth-century Edinburgh can be sensed from the story of Jessie King who gained notoriety as the 'Stockbridge baby farmer' and died on the gallows in the Old Calton Jail in 1889. The last woman murderer to be executed in the city, she aroused public anger and a certain sympathy because she revealed a side to Edinburgh which those in society chose to ignore or were perhaps genuinely unaware of – the selling off of unwanted children by parents.

Jessie King and her lover Pearson lived in Dalkeith Road. A young woman, Elizabeth Campbell, who worked in a wire factory gave birth to a son Walter and before she died in post-delivery complications named the father as David Finlay of Leith. Finlay decided the baby should be adopted and Jessie King told him she had recently lost a child. He swallowed her story, and paid her £5 to take the child. At first King and Pearson appeared perfectly happy with the new family set-up. One day, however, Pearson returned home to find the child missing and Jessie said she had taken him to an orphans' home because she was tired of him.

In May 1887 another unmarried woman, Catherine Gunn, a domestic, bore twin sons, Alexander and Robert, whom she fostered to a woman in Rose Street. King and Pearson had moved to Stockbridge, taking rooms in the name of Macpherson. When an advertisement appeared offering the twins for adoption Jessie was one of twenty-eight applicants. She was given Alexander along with an adoption fee of £3. She told her landlady the boy's mother was her husband's sister. The young woman she employed as a child-minder while she worked in the local laundry was told by Jessie one day that the boy's father had taken him back. When Alexander's mother tried to see him, she found the 'Macphersons' had moved house.

Jessie King then took over the custody of another child, born in August 1888. Violet Tomlinson's mother was in domestic service and like the Gunn woman could not afford to keep her baby. When Jessie spun a story about being unable to have a

The view from the Colonies – across the Water and beyond the Grange Cricket Ground to the spire of Fettes College, another educational endowment by a rich Edinburgh businessman.

baby herself and not being interested in the amount of the fee itself, a sum of £2 was agreed. King was seen returning with the child to the house in Cheyne Street which she and Pearson rented after their sudden move from Ann's Court after the disappearance of Alexander. But no one ever saw Violet alive again and Pearson said he was unaware King was looking for another child. There seemed to be no curiosity about the disappearance of a child in those days, but on Friday, October 26, 1888 the hypocrisy was unveiled by a terrible discovery. A group of lads playing in Cheyne Street found a parcel wrapped up in a waterproof coat on waste ground. They kicked it around for a while, and when curiosity got the better of two of them they started to unwrap it – and discovered a decomposing body.

The police were informed; Dr Littlejohn, the same medical officer, was called and identified the body as that of a boy, about a year old. Round the child's neck was a ligature.

Police inquiries uncovered the sudden disappearance of Violet Tomlinson about a month earlier, and Detective Inspector James Clark questioned Jessie King. His suspicions aroused, the inspector decided to search the Cheyne Street house. In a coal cupboard, apparently normally kept locked, he found a small body wrapped in canvas. Dr Littlejohn identified a baby girl who had been strangled. King was charged with the murders of Alexander Gunn and Violet Tomlinson and confessed she had strangled the boy, claiming she had tried unsuccessfully to have him placed in the orphans' home. She had wrapped the body in cloth and kept it in a cupboard, taking it to both houses in Stockbridge before she dumped it on waste ground.

She claimed that when she brought Violet home the baby was crying and she gave her some whisky to calm her. But the child started gasping for air and King covered her mouth and choked her. Then she tied a cloth over Violet's mouth and put the body in the coal-hole.

Further police inquiries revealed the story of Walter Campbell, and the industrious Inspector Clark had the Dalkeith Road flat searched and the floor boards lifted – but no body was found. A third charge of murder against King was dropped by the Crown.

Pearson appeared to be genuinely in the dark about the woman's secret deeds and co-operated fully with the police. King went to trial at the High Court on Feburary 18, 1889 and the defence counsel could do little but attack those parents prepared to pay a fee to be unburdened of their children. The inevitable verdict came quickly from the jury and King faced her equally inevitable sentence of death from a black-capped Lord Justice-Clerk.

Surely even the discreet breakfast rooms of the New Town must have echoed with the reactions the 'baby farmer' generated.

Further along the Water, one of the best known districts of Stockbridge is known as the Colonies, the rows of symmetrically laid-out houses in the 'Whins' where David Roberts played as a boy. The houses were built as a major social experiment by the Edinburgh Co-Operative Building Company, formed in 1861. The aim was to provide housing at

reasonable cost for the artisan classes, and the majority of the initial shareholders were in the building trade, mostly stonemasons. The land on the river bend was feued in 1861 and work started on the first houses in Reid Terrace.

As they were sold the money was ploughed back into further building and more terraces were started. At one stage construction became spasmodic and it was not until 1911 that the entire layout was completed. It forms, like the other Colony developments in the city, a group of particular architectural interest, one special feature being the outside stairs leading to the upper-level houses. The houses also have many beautifully carved stones depicting not only masonic signs, but giving details of completion dates. Alongside the housing development lay the Canonmills distillery, and it seems incredible in view of the success and popularity enjoyed by the Colonies as a purely domestic area that as recently as 1977 the residents had to organise a vigorous defence to protect themselves from a proposed warehousing and industrial development after the distillery was demolished. Thankfully, the major part of the site was eventually given over to modern housing filling the gap in Glenogle Road.

On the other side of the Water from the Colonies is Rocheid Path, a tree-lined glade which cuts through to Tanfield. The name comes from the Rocheid family who acquired Inverleith Estate in 1665 and built the 'new' Inverleith House, now the central feature of the Royal Botanic Garden.

When James Rocheid wanted to build the new mansion house and enclose the estate in the 1770s, he was entitled by law to charge three-quarters of the cost of the work to his heir, his brother Captain John Rocheid of the Royal North British Dragoons. The total cost of the work was £4109.4s.11d, and the brother was faced with a bill for £3081.18s.8¼d. The captain was not prepared to meet that figure and the argument went to court, with judgement given in 1778 against the younger man by Sir Archibald Cockpen, the Depute Sheriff of Edinburgh. What makes the judgement so fascinating, however, is that it outlines in minute detail the building of the new mansion, the materials used, the price paid to each sub-contractor, even the price of nails and tiles.

James Rocheid planned 'to build a new mansion house on his said entailed lands/the former having become ruinous by length of time/and to erect a compleat set of offices or repair such of the old offices as would answer the purpose. To inclose with a stone wall the West parts of his said entailed lands and Estate lying next to Drylaw ground the same being presently possessed by Thomas Veitch. To lift the North Walls of Inverleith Parks near the High Road leading from Leith to Queensferry and build the same closs to the said road. To inclose with a stone dyke and sunk fence the grounds of the Haugh part of the said estate presently possessed by the said Thomas Veitch . . .' Among the tradesmen's costs was 'to five days and a half of a marble cutter squaring and setting the (Dutch white) tyles at two shillings and six pence per day . . .' James Watson, wright in Canonmills, and David Anderson, the architect who supervised the building, had entered contracts for the house to be completed by August 1, 1776. From the lawn at the house is one of the finest views of Edinburgh to the north.

We noticed the re-introduction of the Riding of the Marches higher up the Water of Leith at Currie, but the villagers of Stockbridge saw in 1717 what Maitland in his history describes as the last such ceremony in Edinburgh: 'The Magistrates and Common Council, attended by the principal Citizens and chief Officers belonging to the Town, together with the Bailiffs (bailies) and chief Officers of the Town of Leith, and Districts of the Canongate, Portsburgh, and Potterrow; the Officers of the City, train'd bands and proper Bands of Musick, all sumptuously apparelled, and mounted on stately Horses well accoutred, formed a long and pompous Cavalcade'. Maitland says they came by 'Canonmills to Stockbridge, and crossing the Water, proceeded to Dean, and back by the Water of Leith, thence to Drumsheugh and St Cuthbert's Churchtown; thence winding Eastward along the Northern Side of the Nordlock to its Eastern Extremity, and returning back to St Cuthbert's marched back to Edinburgh which they entered through the West Port'.

That polluted mill lade on the northern side of the river so strongly criticised on health grounds took power into the hamlet of Silvermills, once a secluded beauty spot in open

This old rustic bridge leading from Rocheid Path into the Colonies was rebuilt at the end of 1977, and still provides a handy shortcut for residents.

countryside. According to Robert Chambers, the name is derived from part of an abandoned plant designed to melt silver ore discovered in 1607 in Linlithgowshire, while Sir Daniel Wilson in his *Memorials* suggests the village 'may not improbably owe its origin to some of the alchemical projects of James IV or V, both of whom were greatly addicted to the royal sport of hunting for the precious metals with which the soil of Scotland was then believed to abound'. However, the village occupants in the nineteenth century were primarily occupied as tanners. Recently there has been concern in town-planning circles to control development in the Silvermills area bounded by Henderson Row, Hanover Street, Fettes Row and Clarence Street, and to encourage small workshops to redevelop a working village atmosphere.

From Silvermills the mill lade divided, one part going direct to Canonmills Loch and the other curving in front of Fettes Row before also going to the Loch.

In Glenogle Road, a short run of steps is one of the few remnants of Gabriel's Road, once one of the best-known walkways in the town, stretching from beside Register House down to Inverleith House. Its route took it past the east end of Abercromby Place and down to Cumberland Street, then turned west to Silvermills and Glenogle Road before crossing the Water on stepping stones. According to Chambers, 'when the fields upon which the New Town is now built flourished in their pristine condition, Gabriel's Road was a common place of assignation for lovers: and the sweet hawthorn hedges which formerly skirted it have shed their summer fragrance over many a happy scene of earnest passion and light-hearted badinage'.

The 'merry lairds' of Inverleith often reeled home down the road and faced the hurdle of the stepping stones before they got safely into their abode.

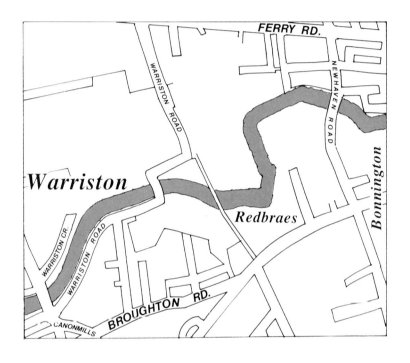

CHAPTER 8

Canonmills to Bonnington

The mills at Canonmills were built by King David I for the Augustinian canons of Holyrood for use of their vassals, thus giving their name to one of the oldest of the Water of Leith villages. Two old granary buildings in Canon Street and a stone lintel at the petrol station can still be seen as a reminder of a long history and, again, of a village so long in the country. It came within the old Barony of Broughton, the 'toun' which lay up the slope to the south. The Incorporation of Baxters of the Canongate were thirled to have their corn ground at Canonmills or pay a sum in compensation.

For many years the Water of Leith, at one time described as 'the great river' and certainly wider and deeper in some stretches than we know it now, was the effective northern boundary for the city. It was fordable, but only at low water, and in Court of Session papers in 1767 there is mention of 'the new bridge at Canonmills'. The present three-arch bridge was built in 1840, and rebuilt in 1896.

Canonmills was obviously an important part of the city's life, and in addition to the flour mills it had a playing card manufactory, and the distillery owned by the Haig family.

Peter de Bruis in 1681 petitioned the Privy Council for a monopoly to make playing cards at his factory, and the Lords granted his request. They prohibited 'all merchant and other persones whatsomever to import, vend, sell or make use of in this kingdome any playing cards after the first day of April next except those made by the said Peter Bruis'.

This instruction was not kindly accepted by Bruis's rivals, and he complained to the Privy Council that his mill had been demolished and that the complainant Alexander Hunter had also thrown his wife into the dam and sworn at her. Hunter was fined £50 and sent to prison. Bruis in his evidence claimed that his enemies 'did under silence and cloud of night come to the said paper milne, and there most maliciously and individuously breake doune the same and render her altogether useless'. He also alleged they 'did divert the water from the said milne when she was set agoeing by opening the sluices and withdrawing the water'. They 'had also invaded and abused the complainer's wife and servants, and threw dust in their faces, and threw the complainer's wife in the milne dame and committed several other outradges'. There were several other incidents which conspired to make Bruis feel he was not wanted in Canonmills and in 1683 he moved his business to the West of Scotland.

One of the most tumultuous events occurred in 1784 when a hunger riot took place because of the scarcity of food in Edinburgh. A rumour spread that the Haig family who were distillers at Canonmills were using oats and potatoes in their processing, and this to the mob was a wrong use of much-needed food. A crowd went down the hill to the Haigs' mill but were driven off by the workmen. The Riot Act had to be read by Sheriff Baron Cockburn, father of Lord Cockburn. A few days later the mob tried again, but the military were ready for them and charged to break them up. Two of the rioters were subsequently whipped through the streets and sentenced to fourteen years' transportation.

The village of Broughton lay in the area now ringed by Albany Street, Broughton Place, Dublin Street and Barony Street and was in its time a power of its own, with a Tolbooth and court in the centre of the village.

Chambers describes it in 1825 as having 'irregular groups of little cottages, hemmed closely in on all hands by the encroaching limits of the wide-spread capital. This is said to be a place of great antiquity, and was once a burgh of regality, with magistrates, who had power of life and death'.

From the village square a path led down to the river at Canonmills, while Broughton Loan brought the worthy citizens on an afternoon stroll into the countryside. As part of the growing New Town, however, the old village was brought into the Royalty of the city in 1786 and its distinctive appearance has long since vanished. There is now no trace either of the Broughton Burn which sprang up in front of what is Mansfield Place and crossed the nursery grounds behind Gayfield House to Bonnington Road. It ran in an open ditch, and while it was fairly clear in Edinburgh in 1872, a public health report said that once in Leith the burn suffered from privy discharges, cow house refuse, human filth and animal remains.

It's a continuing battle to keep rubbish out of the river – and it's been going on for years, as this 1975 scene near Canonmills Bridge shows. Regularly various groups, including schoolchildren, organise clean-ups on different stretches, but for too many citizens the Water of Leith is merely a dumping ground.

The Canonmills Loch lay in the hollow between Royal Crescent and Eyre Place, a shallow and marshy pool. Where Eyre Crescent now stands was Canonmills House.

When the Canonmills Loch below Royal Crescent was drained the ground was for a time the site of one of Edinburgh's most popular attractions – the Royal Patent Gymnasium. It was constructed by John Cox of Gorgie and opened in April 1865. It included a 'rotary boat' or 'great sea serpent', a circular boat about fifteen feet in diameter with seats for 600 rowers. It circled a centre post. There was also a giant see-saw 100 feet long by seven feet broad, rising fifty feet at the ends, and trapezes, canoes, small velocipedes and boneshakers.

This restored building is one of the last traces of milling at Canonmills
– on the wall is a metal plaque with the inscription 'The Canon Mill'.
On the roof are carvings of birds and animals.

'Here, too, are a vast number of vaulting and climbing poles,
rotary ladders, stilts, spring-boards, quoits, balls, bowls, and
little boats and canoes on ponds, propelled by novel and
amusing methods. In winter the ground is prepared for skaters
on a few inches of frozen water, and when lighted up at night
by hundreds of lights, the scene, with its musical accessories, is
one of brightness, gaiety, colour and incessant motion', says a
contemporary report. An advertisement described the
gymnasium as 'The Increasing Wonder of Edinburgh' with
bands on Saturdays and Sundays.

Canonmills, as the city grew, was leap-frogged for some time
by the New Town developers pushing houses into Howard
Place, Warriston Crescent and Inverleith Row. The incomers
found, however, that they were cut off from some of the
conveniences of life in the Old Town and the Princes Street
areas. So in 1835 some of them applied to the Sheriff to have a
stance for sedan chairs and for porters at the north end of
Canonmills Bridge.

The stone with the words 'The Baxters land 1686' is now incorporated into a brick wall at the petrol station at Canonmills.

The Sheriff gave permission, limiting the number of chairmen for the stance to four. Because it was thought there would not be sufficient business for full-time employment as chairmen, they were also allowed to act as porters. Four regular porters were also permitted at the stance, but they in turn were not to be chairmen unless they joined the Society of Chairmasters and Bearers of Edinburgh, or received a special licence for the Society's council.

'The four porters and four chairmen when not engaged in carrying a chair were to wear an apron and have at least four fathoms of rope by their side, and the town badge upon their breast, with their number and name engraved on them. They were likewise each to have on their stand two creels, one for coal, and the other for bottles. They were as usual to be bound to render assistance at a fire or disturbance, and to give immediate notice to the police of every person whom they should discover stealing goods, or mugging coals from carts or horse loads, or who might be concerned in smuggling liquor. It was also strictly enjoined that no drink money or gratuity

Puddocky – the stretch of the Water of Leith between Canonmills and Warriston gets its nickname from the hamlet of Paddock Hall which formerly stood on its banks.

whatever was to be asked or received by those on the stance, from anyone newly entertaining as a chairman or porter.'

In addition to the usual rates, it was laid down that 'for bath-chairs placed on wheels and hurled by one man' the fare should be two-thirds only. The chairmen were fighting a losing battle against the coach, however, and by the 1860s the trade had vanished from the city streets.

Almost a century earlier, Hugo Arnot in his 1788 history recounts of the chairmen: 'The street chairs are to be had on a minute's warning, at all hours of the night or day. The fare is very reasonable; the chairmen are all Highlanders; and they carry the chairs so much better than the Irish chairmen of London, that an inhabitant who visits the metropolis can hardly repress his laughter at facing the aukward rabble of a street-chair in the city of London'.

Heriot Hill House, originally built in 1788, still stands at the corner of Broughton Road, and the old school building attended by Robert Louis Stevenson is now turned into a place of worship for members of the former Dublin Street Baptist Church whose mission hall the Canonmills building was for many years.

The river passes – and in the past has flooded – the dog racing track and kennels at Powderhall. The stadium is likely to face a major redevelopment after being sold in 1988.

The *Scots Magazine* for 1765 records: 'On Monday, November 25, an Antipaedobaptist administered the ordinance of baptism to two adults in the Water of Leith, hard by Canonmills, near Edinburgh in the following manner: The two persons being first stripped, were cloathed with long black gowns, and then went into the water along with their minister, who, after repeating some words in their ordinary form, took them by the nape of the neck, plunged them down over head and ears and kept them for a little while wholly under the water'.

The Water was frequently used for baptism, and in 1652 the diarist John Nicoll records that thrice weekly believers were 'dippit at Bonnington Mill, betwixt Edinburgh and Leith both men and women of good rank. Some days there would be sundry hundred persons attending that action'.

Public baptism has come back into fashion, and at least one Edinburgh church is now using the sea at Silverknowes for the ceremony. Across the water in Tanfield Lane, now being developed as a huge insurance office block, stood two rival gas companies. On the south side of the lane was the Oil Gas Company of which Sir Walter Scott was chairman. It failed in 1839 and the site became the Tanfield Hall to which the seceders from the Church of Scotland marched from the General Assembly in St Andrew's Church, George Street, in 1843 under the leadership of Dr Thomas Chalmers to form the Free Kirk. On the north side were the Portable Gas Works whose gasometers were for long a familiar sight.

At Canonmills occurred one of the most embarrassing moments for Edinburgh Town Council when they missed the arrival of Queen Victoria.

Lord Justice-Clerk Sir J.H.A. Macdonald tells how for the first visit to Scotland of the Queen in 1842 he and his sister were taken to a grandstand in what was then a grazing field between Pitt Street (now Dundas Street) and Brandon Street. 'I can recall the exact location of it by having seen through the space between the floor boards the filthy sewage-laden mill stream taken from the Water of Leith, and carried along the back of Moray Place on to Canonmills, after serving the mills at Stockbridge'.

That visit was to prove a most shame-faced one for the Lord Provost Sir James Forrest and his councillors, who were expected to present the keys of the city to the Queen at Canonmills where a mock gate was erected. The crowds were amazed and then very much amused when the Royal procession suddenly appeared and swept through the gateway without any official welcome. It turned out there had been a breakdown in communication between Sir Robert Peel, the minister in attendance, and the city officials who had not expected the Royal entourage to leave their yacht at Granton so soon after breakfast.

Within hours the town was rocking to a ditty to the tune of 'Hey, Johnny Cope':

> Hey, Jamie Forrest, are ye waukin' yet?
> Or are yer bailies snorin' yet?

The councillors had tried to make amends when they got word in the City Chambers of the Queen's early entry, but by then

Chancelot Mill, built in 1892 for the Scottish Co-operative Wholesale Society, once dominated the landscape. But the building, off Ferry Road, was closed in 1969 and subsequently badly damaged by fire. Its site is now covered by housing.

she was well on her way to Dalkeith Palace. Later the Queen consented to a proper official entry and the decorated gate was taken up to the High Street for the ceremony.

The lands of Warriston stretched to the river bank, and in the elegant Warriston Crescent the composer Frederic Chopin visited No. 10 as a guest of Dr Lyschinski, a Polish homoeopathic doctor who had settled in Edinburgh. It is recorded that the musical genius found himself somewhat bored with the attentions of the young Edinburgh ladies who wanted his opinion on their music-making. To mark Chopin's visit, however, an annual concert is still held in the house where he stayed.

From those houses originally was a splendid view to the Golden Acres and the orchards and strawberry gardens for which Canonmills was well known:

> Canonmills
> Where young folk gang to get their fills
> Of curds and cream, and fine gooseberries,
> Apples, pears and geans, and cherries.

In the House of Warriston in 1600 took place one of the most haunting of Scottish murders. The estate was at that time in the possession of the Kincaid family. In July of that year the townsfolk were rocked by the death of the master. As Robert Birrel, a burgess, recorded in his diary: 'John Kincaid of Waristone murderit be hes awin wyff and servant man and her nurische being also upon the conspiracy. The said gentilwoman being apprehendit, scho wes tane to the Girth Crosse upon the 5 day of Julii, and her heid struk frae her bodie at the Cannagait fit; quha diet verie patiently. Her nurische was brunt at the same tyme, at 4 houres in the morneing, the 5 of Julii'. Missing from that account is the horse-boy Robert Weir who fled and was not taken into custody until four years later when the full tale of the murder was revealed.

The Laird of Warriston, John Kincaid, was married to Jean Livingstone and the marriage turned sour, leading to the young bride's physical ill-treatment. Her nurse, Janet Munro, is said first to have put the idea of revenge into her mistress's mind and the idea of disposing of the laird was formulated. Weir was hidden in a cellar until midnight and then went with

At Stedfastgate on the walkway stands this monument built with stones from the Catherine Sinclair fountain which stood at the junction of Princes Street and Lothian Road until 1932. It was put in store and the monument was constructed to mark the centenary of the Leith Battalion of the Boys' Brigade whose motto is 'Sure and Stedfast'.

Lady Warriston up to the chamber where Kincaid was 'tackand the nychtis rest'. Weir struck the man, knocked him out of bed and kicked him. When Kincaid cried out, Weir seized him by the throat and strangled him.

According to Jean, she had left the room before the fatal deed, and when Weir emerged he rejected her plea to take her away with him. When the news of the Laird of Warriston's death was known, Jean, the nurse Munro and two servants were arrested and taken to the Tolbooth. Their trial took place 'within three suns' and Lady Warriston, the nurse and one of the women servants were convicted.

Jean was granted the comparative concession of being beheaded by the Maiden, the Scottish version of the guillotine, at the foot of the Canongate. But even at four in the morning a big crowd had gathered to see her meet her fate. Janet Munro and the 'hyred woman' were strangled and burned at the stake on Castle Hill at the same time.

The trial of Robert Weir took place on June 26, 1604, and after the inevitable verdict he was ordered to be 'tane to ane skaffold to be fixt besyde the Croce of Edinburgh, and thair to be broken upoune ane Row [wheel] quhill [until] he be deid'.

Then his body was to be set up in a public place between 'Warestoun' and 'the toun of Leyth'. The punishment of breaking a man on a wheel was particularly gruesome and was used to impress on everyone the severity of the charge.

Birrel's diary succinctly recorded the execution: 'Robert Weir broken on ane cartwheel, with ane coulter of ane pleuche [plough] in the hand of the hangman, for murdering of the guidman of Warriston . . .'

The stretch which runs downstream from Canonmills is known locally as Puddocky, not as has been suggested because young boys used to hop like frogs across the stepping stones which were there, but because a hamlet called Paddock Hall nestled there. There are several references to the little community, and to the 'ford at Puddocky'.

On the northern bank stands the Warriston Cemetery which was opened in 1843, originally as the Edinburgh Cemetery. It was intended to be in the 'pleasure ground' style, and has some fascinating Gothic sculptures, but in recent years has fallen prey to vandals who have overturned and otherwise damaged many fine stones.

The village of Warriston and the farm of Warriston Mains – for this was lush pastureland – stood at the Warriston Road entrance to the cemetery.

At the turn of the century the right bank of the Water below Canonmills was occupied by 'marble yards, lithograph works, steam laundries, football and recreation grounds, railway sidings and nursery gardens' and great crowds gathered in Logie Green or Powderhall for the athletic events of the time, including a Scottish Cup Final between Hearts and Hibs. A number of manor houses were situated here, stretching from Heriot Hill to Pilrig with Logie Green, Beaverbank, Blandford House, Old Broughton Hall, Powderhall, Rosebank, Stewartfield and Redbraes among them. Pilrig House has recently been converted with great finesse into highly desirable flats.

The city cleansing department's works at Powderhall were once dominated by a great chimney, now taken down, and it stood on the site of an old gunpowder factory. In 1695 James Balfour was one of the men given the right to manufacture gunpowder north of the Border. Dominating the other side of

The demolition of the listed Bonnington Mill buildings and the redevelopment of the site was strongly resisted by amenity and other groups. But the fight was finally lost in 1983. Bonnyhaugh House was one of the few original buildings to be retained.

the river was the massive Chancelot Mill, whose clock tower was a familiar and important part of the local scene.

The river is in placid mood as it winds between Logie Green and Bonnington around the green area of St Mark's Park. The walkway itself avoids the undulations and runs past the flourishing allotment colonies which run down from Warriston Crematorium site onto the old railway line. The Chancelot site is now covered with housing, and the developers have also all but covered the milling lands of the next community of importance – Bonnington.

Bonnington still has a mill wheel to depict its antecedents, albeit it stands at the entrance of the new housing estate. The lands and mills of Bonnington or Bonnytoun were part of the Barony of Broughton and were included in King David's confirmation charter to the Abbey of Holyrood in 1143.

Crossing the river until the early eighteenth century was by stepping stones only, and at that time two communities nestled by the stream. The mills and their adjoining cottages were on the south, and tenant farmers had their 'toun' on the other bank. A wooden footbridge constructed largely to assist the Newhaven fishwives carrying their heavy loads on the direct route to the Old Town of Edinburgh came into use, linking the hamlets into a village.

The ford at Bonnington was regarded as safe, giving gentle access from the banks which were very steep downstream. The village suffered in 1544 when the Earl of Hertford's English troops arrived in the Forth and disembarked at Wardie Tower and Granton Craigs before marching to the Water of Leith. A small Scottish force was waiting at Bonnington Mills, but it gave way and the Englishmen crossed safely and headed towards Leith, having to cross the Broughton Burn and deal with some other Scottish forces en route.

The village and mill at Bonnington were destroyed, and the community suffered the same fate after the Scottish defeat at the Battle of Pinkie in 1547. The millers and their families were used to violence, so typical of the times. In September 1620, John Russell, the Leith historian, states: 'Sir Patrick Moneypenny of Pilrig with some of his tenants and servants attacked Bonnington Mills [there were now two] and threatened 'to lay the same waiste' for which riotous conduct the Privy Council imprisoned Moneypenny in Edinburgh Castle. The Logans of Bonnington were even more turbulent. George Logan, with his son Robert, and numerous kinsmen in Leith, carried on a bitter feud with the Kincaids of Warriston, whose lands marched with Bonnington on the west'.

The Logans and Kincaids, whose young laird at the time was the son of the murderess Jean Livingstone, appeared to have 'daylie made provocation one to another', and in due course both families were ordered to appear before the Privy Council and give assurance of 3000 merks until January 1, 1608 that they would keep the King's peace. This order had followed an incident related in a petition from George Logan and his son Robert who said that when coming 'fra the Place and Manor of Bonnington to the toun of Leith' they were fiercely set upon by Patrick Kincaid, tutor (guardian of the young laird) at Warriston and others, and were wounded 'to the effusion of our blude in grite quantitie and perall of ourlyveis'.

The old mill wheel is a reminder of the bustling days at Bonnington, with the somewhat curtailed or missing chimney stacks on the now flatted Bonnyhaugh House a reminder of what might have been.

The Logans took revenge, and a series of sparring encounters ensued until the Privy Council directive, although the feud continued to be pursued as fiercely as ever. In January 1607 the two families had to lodge assurances of 5000 merks, but following another immediate clash the Council put the ringleaders on either side in prison. In August 1608 representatives of both families pledged themselves for £1000 sterling that the fighting would be over.

There were also civil disputes over the route from Edinburgh to Newhaven, via Broughton or Bonnington. A pamphlet in March 1763 points out that 'there has been constant intercourse, by this common highway, to Newhaven for centuries, since ever Newhaven has been inhabited'. The cause for concern was the decision in August 1762 of Mrs Rannie, 'tenant in the lands of Bonnington, on the north side of the Water of Leith, at the ford at Bonnington mills, [to] attempt to stop the said highway, coming out of the ford, to the new turnpike road; which she did, by casting up deep ditches across the said common highway'.

A complaint was presented to the justices of the peace and Mrs Rannie was ordered to level the ditches. In a subsequent hearing in the case one of the witnesses was Thomas Peacock 'aged 35 years, married, innkeeper in Newhaven', where the Peacock Inn still exists. His evidence included the statement that the inhabitants of Newhaven, the fishing village on the seashore, 'in the summer time send their horses, and other cattle, to be watered at the said ford, that being a common practice in the summer time; and that the inhabitants of Newhaven used likewise to bring water for the use of their families from thence; and that he himself has frequently brought water from that place for his own use in hogsheads or smaller vessels, or carts, by the said road; and that the reason for this practice was, they had no fresh water nearer them . . .'

The occupant of Bonnington mansion house from 1741 was Alexander Le Grand, subsequently a Commissioner of the Customs in Scotland, who keenly supported the introduction of the new Ferry Road by gifting to the Road Trustees the portions of his rich farmlands through which it would run. Previously the rough 'antient road from North Leith to Queensferry' went by Bonnington and Warriston, passing near a 'steep and dangerous precipice' above the Water to the hamlet of Bangholm, near Goldenacre, another rich pastoral area as its name indicates.

The old Bonnington Bridge was built in 1812, and the present bridge, sporting the crests of both Edinburgh and Leith, in 1902-3. Bonnyhaugh House, which still stands amidst its modern housing surrounds, was built by Edinburgh Town Council in 1621, four years after they purchased the mills at Bonnington.

The council had enticed from Holland Jeromias van der Heill, a dyer, to teach his craft in Edinburgh, and set him up in the house. But it seems to have been 1723 when the house and the adjoining bleachfield was first named Bonnyhaugh after being bought by Gilbert Stewart. A notable occupant in later years was Bishop Keith, author of the *Catalogue of Scottish Bishops*, who died in the house in 1757. The river at this point was also used for baptism as we have seen: 'In the days when the sectaries ran riot, the neophytes of adult baptism, including great ladies of the West Country, were brought hither, in cold winter weather, to be 'dippit in the clear rynnand water".

There was a desperate fight by conservation and other bodies to save something of the mill buildings and the seat of Bonnington's history in recent years as the inevitable development plans came forward. In general, they were of little avail, and the new housing down to the waterside has obliterated much tangible history.

Below the bridge a jumble of industrial buildings hems in the Water of Leith as it gets a sniff of the salt sea ahead, and from West Bowling Green Street bridge (built 1889 by the Council of Leith 'aided by some of the neighbouring proprietors') the river is penned upstream by stone and concrete walls before it sweeps into the recreation area of Coalie Park and down to the old harbour of Leith. It passes too that group of housing which stands in The Quilts, a name derived from the French word 'quille', meaning bowls. In the sixteenth and seventeenth centuries twelve acres outside the town wall on the banks of the Water were used by Leithers for sports including bowls, real tennis and skittles. French troops stationed in the area in the sixteenth century had used the word 'quille' for skittles, and this was changed locally into quilts.

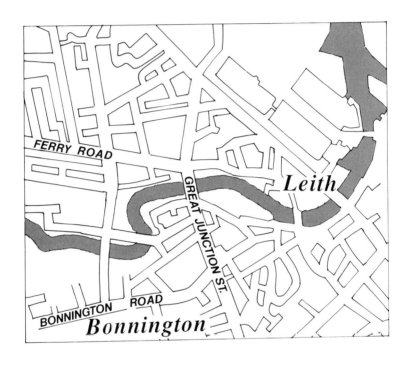

FERRY ROAD

GREAT JUNCTION ST.

Leith

BONNINGTON ROAD

Bonnington

CHAPTER 9

Leith

The mouth of the Water of Leith is now a placid basin alongside the Shore, and surrounded by the new prosperity of the old town. Buildings are being converted with welcome enthusiasm to new, much sought-after riverside housing; flat windows beckon onto the water, and the Yuppie image of London's docklands stands comparison – although the prices here have not yet hit the metropolis giddiness.

The bustle of the old harbour has been swept away with the expansion over almost two centuries of a dockland, and the original wharves and alas too many historic buildings have vanished.

The first mention of Leith is recorded, says Maitland, in the foundation charter of Holyrood Abbey in 1128. It is referred to as Inverleith, the mouth of the Water of Leith. J.C. Irons, in his *Leith and Its Antiquities,* adds that certain grants made in the charter mention Leith 'together with the town of Broughton and its respective divisions, the lands of Inverleith in the neighbourhood of the harbour, with the said harbour, half of the fishings and titles of several fisheries belonging to the Church of St Cuthbert'. The lands of Inverleith are believed to have belonged to the ancient family, the Leiths of Leithhall, who owned Restalrig. The 'Inver' was dropped, certainly early in the thirteenth century – there is reference to Thomas de Restalric making a grant of tenements which he describes as being south of the High Street and between Edinburgh and Leith. And in 1264 there is record of trade between Leith and Inverness – 'for carriage of 548 cattle to Leith by ship'.

It was King Robert the Bruce in his charter of May 8, 1329 who 'gives, grants and in feufarm demits, and confirms to the burgesses of the burgh of Edinburgh, his foresaid burgh of Edinburgh, together with the harbour of Leith, mills, and other pertinents which used justly to be long to them in the reign of King Alexander, his Majesty's predecessor, last deceased, for payment of fifty-two merks yearly'.

Towards the end of that century Logan of Restalrig, whose

Another moment in the walkway's progress. Lord Provost Tom Morgan thanks Mr John McCracken of the Scottish Development Agency for their contribution to the completion of the Coalie Park section in 1982.

property ran along the southern shore of the river, granted Edinburgh the first right to any property connected with Leith Harbour. On May 31, 1398 his charter 'gave, granted, and confirmed to his neighbours, the burgesses, and community of the city of Edinburgh, free power, faculty, and licence, of casting and carrying away the earth and gravel lying upon the bank or shore of the Water of Leith, for enlarging and lengthening their port of Leith, whenever and as often as they pleased, and for placing and making a bridge over the said Water of Leith, within and upon his lands whenever they should think fit; to fix their anchors or other tackling whenever they pleased, without said port'. Logan also granted passage through his lands of Restalrig and town of Leith, with power to the council to make any new road they required. Subsequent enforcement of Edinburgh's rights and powers over the harbour caused great resentment among the merchants and inhabitants of Leith. So much so that in 1806 the Town Clerk, Charles Cunningham, in a report to the council stressing their right to tithe of their property in Leith, told Edinburgh councillors: 'The valuable rights and privileges of the city of Edinburgh, connected with Leith, have never ceased to be viewed with a most jealous eye by the inhabitants of that port, who, from the earliest period of that connection, have made frequent attempts to throw off their vassalage, either by boldly asserting that their independency had been wrested from them by fraud, or by secretly and gradually undermining the influence of the Lord Provost, Magistrates and Town Council. Against attempts of the former kind, the just rights of the city of Edinburgh have always prevailed; but against those of the latter, the mode of attack being secret, the success of the Magistrates and Council has been less decisive'.

The Bruce charter contains reference not only to the harbour but also to the mills. 'The expressions in that old charter are very general, and in all probability were meant to apply to other mills on the Water of Leith', says Mr Cunningham. 'For it appears that at the time the Queen Regent acquired (in 1555) the superiority of Leith from Logan of Restalrig, those mills were then in his possession.'

This fight for its own freedom has persisted in Leith over the centuries – indeed many staunch Leithers can still be found who have little truck with Edinburgh and regard the complete takeover by the city in 1920 against an overwhelming plebiscite for independence as a major catastrophe.

That separate identity is readily seen today in the old Council

A warehouse converted into very des. res. Leith has come storming back into the public's imagination thanks to a vigorous regeneration programme, and riverside living is very much in vogue – thankfully not yet at London prices!

Chambers, Assembly Rooms, Exchange building, hospital (soon to go), consulates and police station – and its own statues to Robert Burns and Queen Victoria.

The subtle difference between a sea faring community and its neighbour up the hill is still to be savoured in the wynds off the Shore, although the 'improvements' have swept away, over this century particularly, much of what could well have been retained.

The success of the town has been based on the harbour, which was solely the banks of the Water of Leith as it entered into the Firth of Forth, and the men who held the rights to the harbour had a goldmine in their hands, as the shrewd councillors in Edinburgh quickly realised when they went to deal with Logan of Restalrig. The Water of Leith flowed across the broad Leith Sands and the channel was necessarily tidal. The river itself could run high or low depending on the season, and its use in the lower stretches depended on the state of the tide.

The occupying English Earl of Hertford ordered a wooden pier to be built in 1544, but when he returned south he also ordered its destruction lest the Scots found it useful in any future campaign. Early in the seventeenth century another wooden pier was erected, and it lasted more than 200 years. Between 1720-30 a stone pier was built, joined to the wooden one, and a small dock was also formed on the west side of the river mouth. Yet despite the hazards of using the harbour, trade flourished and it was a target for the maruading 'auld enemy'. In 1313 the English burned ships in the harbour, and again in 1411 an English fleet descended on Leith.

By 1457 trade had increased to such an extent that the Scottish Parliament passed an Act restricting the 'multitude of saillers'. Although raided on at least three occasions and shipping burned, Leith in the sixteenth century saw flourishing times with trade to the Continent. By 1654, when accurate figures are available, the Customs for the last three months of that year amounted to £404 and the excise to £270. A return of shipping in 1692 shows that Leith had twenty-nine vessels, and trade was conducted with Northern European and Mediterranean ports.

Hugo Arnot, who was himself a Leither, says that in 1777 the Town Council erected an additional stone quay and that upwards of a hundred ships 'can lie conveniently in this port. It is accommodation with wet and dry docks, and other conveniences for ship-building, which is there carried on to some extent, as vessels come to Leith to be repaired from the different quarters of the east coast of Scotland'. He reckoned for the year ending January 5, 1778 that there were fifty-two ships on foreign trade and forty-four on coasting and fishing work.

Among the imports he lists: from Denmark, oats, pease, barley; from Norway, battens, spars, handspikes, tree nails; from Sweden, bar iron, tar, fir timber; from Russia, flax, tallow, feather beds, linens; from Holland came unbound books and wooden clocks; wine came from France, Spain, Portugal and Gibraltar; and from North America ('before the differences with that country') rice and indigo, otter and racoon skins, and rum.

F

Where the royal foot landed – oh happy day! It caused great rejoicing in Leith and Edinburgh when George IV stepped onto the Shore in 1824 and entered into a programme of celebrations masterminded by Sir Walter Scott among others.

Leaving Leith were coals for Denmark; strong beer, glass bottles and printed paper for Norway; coaches and chariots, with braces and harness, to Russia and Poland; porter and more strong beer for the Germans and the Dutch; while Holland also received lead, carpeting and salmon; dried cod fish, still a delicacy there, was sent to Portugal; and there was a tremendous trade to North America which the War of Indepedence sorely hit.

Wine imports at Leith resulted in considerable duties being paid – £25,272 12s. 2d in the year to January 5, 1775 being typical.

'Home grown' foods were also tempting the English markets, in particular the 'exportation' of oysters. 'This article began to be exported for the London market in the year 1773, ' Arnot writes. 'From their beds in the Forth, they are taken to the Medway, and other rivers not distant from London, where they are deposited to fatten for the consumption of the great metropolis.' But he warns in 1778 that greed for money has pushed the total exports up to 8400 barrels – 'Thus it appears, if the oyster banks on the Forth are not dragged more sparingly, this commodity will be speedily exhausted.'

Among the other 'exports' from Leith Harbour were men who left with a great sense of adventure, as well as those who left Scotland with heavy heart.

They included 210 Covenanting souls and another 47 men cleared from the Tolbooths in Edinburgh and Canongate for transfer to the plantations as punishment for their beliefs and crimes. One man successfully escaped, but the others were herded into the bowels of the *Crown*, which sailed with its human cargo from Leith Roads on November 27, 1679. The seas were stormy and the *Crown's* skipper was forced to drop anchor off the Orkneys. But his ship was driven onto rocks and wrecked on the west side of Deerness. More than 200 prisoners were drowned.

Convicts sent to the colony of Australia were also shipped out of Leith, most never to see their homeland or families again in times of rough, hardened justice. But there could have been few who watched the ships leaving the roads in 1696 who did not believe that a great Scottish drama of prosperity with the founding of a new colony on the Isthmus of Panama was about to be realised. The Darien Scheme was funded entirely by Scots to the tune of £400,000 sterling, and the adventurers in their heavily laden ships set off filled with enthusiasm and great hopes of material reward.

When news of their settlement reached Edinburgh on March 25, 1699 it was celebrated with 'the most extravagant rejoicings'. 'Thanks,' says Arnot, 'were publicly offered up to God in all the churches of the city. At a public graduation of students, at which the magistrates, in their formalities, attended, the professor of philosophy pronounced a harangue in favour of that settlement, the legality of which, against all other pretenders, was maintained in their printed theses; and it seems even to have been a common subject of declamation from the pulpit.'

But the Darien Scheme had powerful rivals and the company 'felt severely the influence of its powerful opponents'. 'The petitions and complaints of the company and the parliament, and the murmurs of the people, were equally disregarded. Upon news being received of the defeat of the Spaniards who attacked our settlement, a mob rose, obliged the inhabitants to illuminate their windows, committed outrages upon the houses of those who did not humour them by compliance, secured the avenues to the city, and proceeded to the tolbooth, the doors of which they burnt, and set at liberty two printers who had been confined for printing pamphlets reflecting on the government.'

Leith-sur-Mer is the image with waterside bistros, good restaurants, liberal licensing hours and riverside housing. And this floating restaurant, Ocean Mist, in 1988 brought another touch of maritime flavour at its mooring at the Shore.

'But, when it was understood they were driven from their settlement, their capital lost, and their hopes utterly extinguished, they were seized with a transport of fury. Violent addresses were presented to the King, and the mob were so outrageous, that the Commissioner, and officers of state found it prudent to retire for a few days, lest they should have fallen sacrifices to popular fury,' reports Arnot. Many Scots were financially ruined in the collapse of the Darien Company which had been formed to promote trade with Africa and the Indies, and its calamitous ending had far-reaching repercussions in the country into the eighteenth century.

At least one tragic miscarriage of justice also stemmed directly from the Darien depression and desire in some way to even the score. In April 1705 Captain Thomas Green of the East India ship *Worcester* and two of his crew were found guilty after trial in Edinburgh on what many believed was a trumped-up charge of murder and piracy.

He, his first mate John Madder, a Scot, and sixteen others of the crew were the unfortunate pawns in the clash between the Scottish Parliament and the East India Company who had used their not inconsiderable powers to prevent English merchants investing in the Darien Scheme. The deaths of Green and his shipmates were ordained by the Scots Court of Admiralty. A depleted Privy Council, with a baying Edinburgh mob outside calling for the Englishmen to be strung up, considered Green's appeal, and agreed that the sentence be carried out against only three men – Green himself, Madder, and the gunner Simpson. With the sickening ritual of the day, the public execution was duly carried out at Leith Sands, and the satisfied mob went about their cantankerous business.

Leith Sands played a dramatic part in the life of the citizenry of both Leith and Edinburgh. They were the site of executions and the scenes of great merriment.

The Sands in 1799 saw a party of Highland recruits, due to sail overseas from Leith, dispatched to their deaths after a mutiny. The men refused to embark and took a stand on the shore; twelve of them were killed and others wounded before they caved in.

While an outing for a public execution was considered in those days a matter of pleasure as well as civic duty, the Sands were unquestionably better known and appreciated for horse-racing and other sporting events. Scotland seems to have enjoyed horse-racing from the beginning of the seventeenth century with mention of events at that time in Cupar, Lanark and Hamilton. King James VI certainly encouraged the sport, although during Cromwell's Commonwealth the sport of kings was suppressed. At the Restoration it made a very welcome return.

The wagering gentry of Edinburgh doubtless tried out their horses along the flat sands before the first formal mention of Leith Races in 1661. The *Mercurius Caledonius* reported: 'Our accustomed recreations on the Sands of Leith were much hindered today (Saturday, March 2, 1661) by reason of a furious storm of wind, accompanied by a thick snow, yet we have had some noble gamesters that were so constant at their sport as would not forebeare a designed horse march. It was a providence the wind was from the sea, otherwise they had run

To celebrate the opening of new housing in 1985 an appropriately dressed crew rowed the 'inspecting officer', actor Iain Cuthbertson, into the rivermouth for the ceremonials.

the hazard either of drowning or splitting upon Inchkeith'.

The annual races became a great social event, and there was no more enthusiastic supporter than the most renowned leader of the Edinburgh mob in the eighteenth century, Bowed Joseph from the Cowgate. He, according to Robert Chambers, 'contrived by dint of popular qualifications, to subject the rabble to his command, and to get himself elected by acclamation, dictator of all its motions and exploits'. General Joseph Smith was a cobbler residing 'in some low den' and he was deformed – 'yet this wretch, miserable and contemptible as he appeared, might be said to have had, at one time, the command of the Scottish metropolis'.

Smith's influence was great not least because the town councillors greatly feared and responded to the mob, and he revelled in his power. It must have been a great relief to the magistrates to know that Joseph's instruction 'Now disperse my lads' was enough to quell an impending riot, once he had made his point and obtained his wish.

Joseph had another side to his character – he never allowed his wife to walk beside him, 'it being his opinion that women are inferior to the male part of creation and not entitled to the same privileges'. He made her stride a few paces to his rear, and when he wanted to speak to her he whistled on her like a dog. After hearing what he had to say, she retreated to her accepted station.

Joseph, it was said, could organise a crowd of no fewer than 10,000 by beating his drum and calling them out. Chambers comments: 'It would appear, after all, that there was a moral foundation for Joseph's power ... the little man was never known to act in a bad cause, or in any way to go against the principles of natural justice. He employed his power in the redress of such grievances as the law of the land does not, or cannot, easily reach; and it was apparent that almost everything he did was for the sake of what he himself designated fair play'. He died about 1780, killed by a fall from the top of a Leith stage coach after a day at the races. He had enjoyed his times at the Sands, probably had a few wagers and was certainly the worse of too many drinks doubtless bought by his supporters and the gentry, anxious to be on terms with him. He was hoisted with much merriment onto the stage, but its jostling journey to the city proved his final undoing.

Edinburgh Town Council from early days were patrons of the racing, and their accounts record some of the expenses including drink to the City Guard, fees for coaches to get councillors there, and in August 1735 the cost of an advertisement in the *Caledonian Mercury* – £2 19s.

It was part of Leith Town Clerk's duties to have the course in suitable condition and measured off properly. In 1768 the measurer Alexander Wood reported: 'I have this day measured off one and one-third mile of 2346 yards of ground on the sands and find the distance betwixt the starting to the distant stoop to be 244 yards and from the starting stoop to the first pole to be 293 yards'.

The need to have the Sands in proper order without any obstacles was evident in the Leith magistrates' endeavours to ensure everything went well. A proclamation of July 4, 1787 was typical of their approach to the task: 'The Magistrates do

Leith races – as captured by Walter Geikie, the deaf and dumb
Edinburgh artist whose legacy is a series of superb sketches of city and
Scottish life. Already the backers have their doubts about putting their
cash on this cuddy, and the jockey seems none too certain himself!

strictly prohibite and discharge all persons from digging for
bait, digging for ballace, or making holes for any purpose
whatever in the sands of Leith from the time of publishing
hereof until the races which are to begin upon 19th current
shall be over; and do also prohibite and discharge all persons
from laying down stones or timber or any other thing on the
said sands or on the roads or lanes leading thereto during the
time of the said races, whereby the course in the races or roads
may be obstructed or incumbered, and that under the penalty
of ten pounds Scots for each transgression. Given at Leith the
4th July 1787 years'.

The race week was normally the last in July, or the first in
August, and seemed to attract crowds from well furth of

Edinburgh and Leith. It was then, as now, the fashionable thing to be seen at the races. 'This influx of wealthy and idle people kept the city, during the whole of the race week, in a state of feverish excitation, and converted it into one continued scene of gaiety and dissipation,' writes a contemporary commentator. 'These, again, were contrasted with another class, not less happy, but infinitely worse attired, the mechanics and others, the humbler natives of Auld Reekie, who in mirthful squads kept filing amongst Leith Walk.'

The Races were launched in style, with one of the city officers, in gala dress, walking in procession each morning carrying a pole with a gaily ornamented purse – 'the city purse' – for all to see the winnings to be had. As he marched from the High Street, a town guard drummer followed, beating out a tattoo. As they marched they soon gathered a cheery throng who accompanied them to the Sands for the day's jollity.

For there was plenty to do apart from watching the horses and their riders at full gallop. There were the amusements – 'shows, wheels of fortune, and rowly-powly (a version of ninepins) in endless variety; and last, though not least, whole streets of drinking booths and tents. Suffice to say, that for an entire week the town was one continued scene of racing, drinking, and fighting, and the sports were usually concluded by a general demolition of the booths, and a promiscuous fighting-match amongst those who, in spite of whisky and previous pugilistic encounters, were still able to keep their legs. That anybody, save the most degraded, should have regretted the abolition of these saturnalia may seem rather strange, but nevertheless it is the fact that when these races were transferred to the vastly superior course at Musselburgh, many otherwise sensible men spoke as if a serious blow had been struck at the propriety of the auld toon', says J.C. Irons.

The Races moved to Musselburgh in 1815, the turf courses being preferred to the wet, flat sand. There was a brief resurgence from 1836 until 1856 at Leith, however, before the Magistrates and the Dock Commissioners finally brought down the curtain on more than 200 years of the sport on the Sands, and now the Sands themselves are no more, buried as they were under the dock extensions.

'A burly loon, with sweeping straikes, Is thrang at rowly powly . . .' This form of nine-pins was a great favourite at the races on Leith Sands which attracted all sorts of unseemly characters. The game was eventually banned by the Magistrates of Leith in 1811.

The other sport with which Leith is primarily associated is golf, for on Leith Links the great Scottish pastime flourished for many centuries enjoying royal patronage. At first it was seen as a harmful pursuit: in 1457 in King James II's reign a statute was enacted prohibiting the game because it was interfering with the much more practical – for a country perpetually in arms – craft of archery. Yet the game prospered, for in 1471 and again in 1491 similar ordinances were made. By the start of the sixteenth century, however, the monarch James IV was openly enjoying the game.

It is even said that John Knox, the crusading Reformer, relaxed after delivering one of his Sunday sermons with a game in the afternoon. The East Lothian Golf Book notes: 'Certainly his idea, and the idea of our early Reformers – indeed, we may say, the true Scottish idea of Sunday – was that the early part should be given to worship in the house of God, and that after divine service all were free to indulge in bodily recreation. The old Session and Town Council records, of which we hear so much, dealt chiefly with offenders who neglected worship altogether, and golfed during the 'thyme of preaching or the thyme of sermounes'.' Because some Edinburgh folk neglected their church going, in 1592 and 1593 the Town Council passed bye-laws prohibiting golf completely on Sundays as 'profaning the Sabbath day'. Persistent offenders were fined.

King Charles I was another royal enthusiast for the game, as was the Duke of York (later King James VII and II), and they used the Links during stays at Holyrood. Charles is said to have been playing at Leith when he received first word of the rebellion in Ireland, which, to say the least, must have put him off his stroke. Of James, it is related that he was challenged by two English noblemen to a game, and sought a suitable partner. He found the ideal man in a shoemaker John Paterson, 'the worthy descendant of a long line of illustrious golfers', as Chambers puts it. 'If the two southrons were, as might be expected, inexperienced in the game, they had no chance against a pair, one member of which was a good player . . .' Paterson's efforts were rewarded immediately by a gift of the sum played for.

'The story goes on to say that John was thus enabled to build a somewhat stylish house for himself in the Canongate; on the top of which, being a Scotsman, and having of course a pedigree, he clapped the Paterson arms – three pelicans vulned; on a chief three mullets; crest, a dexter hand grasping a golf club; together with the motto – dear to all golfers – Far and Sure.' However, even Chambers is forced to admit: 'There must be some uncertainty about this tale. The house, the inscriptions, the arms only indicate that Paterson built the house after being a victor at golf . . .' Golfer's Land still stands in the Canongate, and whether true or not, it is a good golfing tale and shows how commoner and king can share a common love.

Something of the smaller wagers and cost of golf in the seventeenth century can be gathered from the notebook kept by Sir John Foulis of Ravelston which records on January 13, 1672 – Lost at golfe with Lyon and Hary Hay £1 4s 0d. March 2 – For three golfe balls 0.15s 0d. April 13 – To the boy who carried my clubs, when my Lord Register and Newbyth was at the Links 0.4s 0d. And for a new club for his son the princely sum of 6s Scots.

A good day was had by all – Geikie's picture, 'Coming from the races', tells it all. Some enjoyed themselves too well, and eventually the drunkenness, rowdiness, gambling and other trouble helped to spell the end for what had been a great occasion.

The 'famed field on Forth's sound shore' saw the establishment in 1744 of the Honourable Company of Edinburgh Golfers under the patronage of the city magistrates. The Company built a club house in 1768, but moved to Musselburgh in the 1830s before going to Muirfield on the East Lothian coast in 1891. To this day the Honourable Company remain one of the most prestigious golf clubs in the world, and their course has been the venue for the Open Championship on a number of occasions.

Another sport also prevailed on the Links – that of cock fighting. This became an immensely popular event and the cockpit in Leith was in 1702 charging 10d for the front row, 7d for the second, and 4d for the third to witness the bloodthirsty scene as the birds were egged on by their screaming backers to an ultimate destruction. The Sands also had a cockpit.

CHAPTER 10

'Better Times Are Now In Store'

Leith harbour has been the scene of many tragedies – indeed it is still not unknown for a driver to take a short cut through the docks, miss a turning and end up in the water. But one event which shook the town of Leith occurred on July 16, 1848 – a Sabbath morn – when no fewer than six lives were lost in a boating accident. Under the heading 'Melancholy Occurence' the *Edinburgh Evening Courant* reported that five women and four men 'had been engaged drinking during Saturday night and yesterday morning in a house in the Coalhill, Leith, and had resolved as a finish to their debauch to enjoy a sail in the Firth'.

'There was either a row, or just high spirits, and the boat overturned throwing the party into the water, and the five women and one man drowned.'

'Throughout the day large crowds assembled at the end of the pier to view the scene of the distressing catastrophe, and moralise over the sad fate of the hapless crew. The melancholy occurrence was also made the theme of observation in the discourses in various churches in Leith; and the event, as may well be imagined, has excited considerable sensation in that town'. The report had a further rejoinder: '. . . and it may be added that most of the unfortunate women led an abandoned life'.

Damning reporting, but the incident sparked off the publication of an eight-page leaflet (price ½d or 3s 6d per 100), 'A warning to the Sabbath-breaker and intemperate'. It is a classic example of both concern for and condemnation of the unfortunate classes in Victorian Edinburgh, and particularly reflects the battle against the admittedly prevalent evils of strong drink.

'A party of five women and four men – the former the abandoned girls of the street; the latter, we believe, seamen, and all of them young – had spent the whole, or nearly the whole, of Saturday night and Sabbath morning in drinking and dissipation. It is too well known that this is the choice and

The old Town Hall building in Queen Charlotte Street now houses Leith Police Station. It is one of the many fine buildings which emphasise the port's long independence as a burgh separate from Edinburgh.

favourite night for such riotous debauchery, more shamefully prevalent in Christian Scotland, with all our professed religion and strict Sabbath-observance, than among any people on the face of the earth. Not withstanding all the vigilance of magistrates and of police, haunts are to be found, in which the means of such riotous debauchery are sold to the worst.'

'Above five o'clock in the Sabbath morning, when the bright sun of July was wakening the worshippers of God to their early devotions, and to their preparations for the solemn services and blessed privileges of the day of God's hallowed rest, this party sallied forth, all, it is supposed, in a state of intoxication; but resolved to prosecute their debauch in the eye of the Sabbath sun, in the sight of the awakening sober population of the town. Some hesitation was expressed by one of the females to proceed farther, unless one of the young men for whom she had a partiality would go with her. He agreed and all of them got into a boat at the head of the harbour.'

'It is presumed their intention was to spend the day in sailing about in the Firth, or on Inchkeith; for they took provision and some bottles of whisky with them. The morning, as will be remembered, was one of the calmest and most beautifully serene which the season of midsummer could witness, Heaven smiled on the earth and sea in serenity . . .'

'These deluded and intoxicated individuals proposed to enjoy it in another way – in defiance of the gracious law of God, in contempt of the customs of their religious neighbours, and in professed and open mockery of all religious habits. As they rowed out of the harbour they roused people from their sleep, and disgusted the early spectator of their conduct, by singing drunken and profane songs . . . They thought not of the daring profanity of their present conduct, or of the danger and destruction which that conduct was certainly preparing for them in the future. Senseless, lawless enjoyment was all their object, and though they had already quaffed of it to the tasteless dregs they would pursue it still.'

'With such resolutions, and in a day of such beauty, 'with hope, such as it was, at the prow, and pleasure, such as they desired it, at the stern,' they rowed out of the harbour; but to most of them that voyage was destined to be short; and to all, that pleasure to encounter a melancholy awakening. They had scarce passed the end of the pier, when one of the men proposed to bathe. Some of the rest, and, we believe, the women, opposed it.'

'The foolish individual, however, persevered, and a struggle took place to prevent him. In the confusion, the majority had tumbled to one side of the boat, which was instantly swamped, and filled with water. The whole five wretched females, in their fright, clung helplessly to each other, and to one of the men, and sank. The other three could swim; and, it seems, that one of them, who accompanied the girl who had expressed a preference for him, got hold of her, and supported her for a little, got her to take hold of the keel of the boat, and urged her to cling to it till he should swim to the shore for assistance.'

The pamphlet explains how boats came out from the shore when the accident was seen and from a foreign vessel in the roads. But before any rescuers could reach the scene 'folly had

Leith Assembly Rooms and the Exchange in Constitution Street are another fine example of public buildings in Leith. Built in 1809-10, and designed by Thomas Brown.

done her work and death had claimed six victims – all the girls and one of the men. The other three escaped, and were rescued and brought to the shore, most of them in a state of exhaustion and stupidity . . . It will be observed, that we have used no delicacy of expression in narrating this shocking and disgraceful event; and we think that such would be sadly displaced . . .'

'This party of profane drunkards proposed to spend the day of rest and religious observance in sinful pleasure, away from the sight of men. But their noisy folly summoned men to witness their fate. They were hurried into eternity, not by storm or tempest, not in the midst of the sea, or on sharp rocks, which they could not avoid; their fate was hurried upon them a few yards from land, in sight, and within hearing, of

those who could not aid them; they died as fools die, by their
own disorderly passions, and in pursuit of sinful indulgence;
they were shameless in their folly, and stand forth as a beacon
to all who are pursuing the same course.'

'But let not these remarks be mistaken. We do not say that
sober men never meet such fate, or that it falls especially on
drunkards, and those who desecrate the Sabbath-day. It is not
confined, indeed, to such; but there is no impropriety or want
of charity in asserting that had the party been sober and in the
discharge of a necessary duty, and on a week-day, they could
not have encountered such a fate in such a place, and in such a
serene sea and sky.'

The broadside concludes: 'We have heard it calculated, that
fully £100,000 are spent in strong drink, annually, in the
public-houses of Leith alone . . . Till some effectual means are
taken to end this fearful abuse such events as this melancholy
one will be frequent. They may be moralized upon for a day by
a few; but they will be unheeded and forgot in the midst of the
same evil influences.'

On a happier note, one of the most spectacular arrivals at
Leith came in 1822 when King George IV accepted an
invitation to visit Edinburgh, an event in which Sir Walter Scott
was a leading figure (and which incidentally sparked off the
everlasting popularity of the tartan for clothing).

It was the first time in 140 years that a king had visited
Scotland, and Edinburgh and Leith were prepared to sink their
differences to put on a remarkable welcome for their monarch.
There was debate on whether the royal landing should take
place at Trinity chain pier or at Leith Harbour, and for a
moment the Leithers became so incensed that they might lose
out that they went so far as to send a petition to the King
himself. And Leith won the day.

'Leith now vied with Edinburgh itself in the magnificence of
its preparations for the reception of His Majesty. A raft was
placed on the south side of the inner harbour, from which a
railed gangway ascended to the quay, where it was decided His
Majesty should land. A wooden platform was also erected from
the landing-place to the end of Bernard Street, where it was
arranged His Majesty was to enter his carriage', says a
contemporary report.

And then there was oil . . . and Leith Docks got a new lease of life as the oilmen headed for the North Sea fields. These American oil ships were pictured in 1973.

'A magnificent triumphal arch was erected at the north end of Bernard Street, and another in Constitution Street, on the line of the royal procession to the capital. Seats were fitted up along the whole extent of the pier, sufficient to accommodate two thousand spectators, and a scaffold was erected upon the drawbridge for the accommodation of ladies and persons of quality. A proclamation was issued by the Magistrates of Leith recommending a general illumination on the evening after the King's landing. In short, nothing was left undone by the Magistrates and inhabitants of Leith that could contribute to the accommodation of His Majesty or the grandeur of the anticipated spectacle.'

The royal squadron arrived in Leith Roads on August 14, but because it was raining heavens hard, the landing was postponed until the next day. 'On the morning of the 15th it ceased to rain, and our revered monarch, as he ascended the deck, beheld the Scottish capital with its towers and palaces basking in the rays of an autumnal sun, and the surrounding country spread out before him in all its loveliness.'

The spectacular welcome and procession went off in great style, to the delight of the onlookers. 'It would be utterly impossible to describe the enthusiastic exclamations which burst forth at this moment from all ranks, and they appeared to give the greatest satisfaction to the King. After the King had rested a few minutes in his carriage, which was an open landau, hung very low, and drawn by eight beautiful bays, the drivers being in state liveries, the whole procession moved slowly towards Edinburgh.'

A cast-iron slab incribed 'Geo IV Rex O Felicem Diem' marks the spot at the Shore where the royal foot touched, and such was the joy of the populace that for some time afterwards annual celebrations were held to mark the event.

While the harbour had its days, measures were being pressed ahead to enlarge and improve the dock area. In 1799 civil engineer John Rennie had been engaged to examine the ground and prepare a scheme for docks and extended piers. He proposed carrying a pier on the east side of the channel to eliminate the bar at the river mouth, and to build docks to the west with a deep water entrance. The latter part was adopted, with a drawbridge positioned at Bernard Street. It was not until 1818 that positive steps were taken on Rennie's other suggestion about the western bank and a short breakwater was built, raising the water level at the river mouth.

This tricky entrance which had bedevilled the harbour since its earliest days continued to cause problems until a scheme was adopted to extend the east pier by 1500 feet to a point about 100 yards west of the Martello Tower. This together with other improvements was completed in 1829, the first pile being driven by Lord Provost Trotter in 1826. Further work during the century saw the Victoria Dock in 1851 and the opening of the Prince of Wales graving dock in 1858. As the docks expanded to the east the old race-coursing sands disappeared under the Albert Dock (formally opened in 1869) and the (Duke of) Edinburgh Dock in 1881. The sea wall running from the east end of the Albert Dock to the old Seafield Toll, which

Welcome, comrades. The Russian cruise ship *Konstantin Simonov* docks at Leith. Soviet ships now make regular calls at Leith on their cruising schedules.

enabled the Edinburgh Dock to be formed, was completed in 1877.

The extensions explain how the old signal tower now stands far from the sea at the Shore. Another old signal tower stood in Tolbooth Wynd, near its junction with the Kirkgate.

In 1812 the first steamboat on the Forth, the *Lady of the Lake*, plied between Leith and Alloa. The introduction of steam brought the deathknell to the old luggers which headed out to the Fife ports and to the smacks which made their often tortuous way between Leith and London.

For a flavour of the harbour scene in the mid-nineteenth century, let's take heed of the notes of John Laurie, a Town Clerk of Edinburgh, who jotted in his diary for March 13, 1861: 'Walked to Leith by Bonnington through the Coalhill and along the shore to the far end of the East Pier. Between 30 and 50 years ago, the old harbour used to be crowded with shipping, that part of it between the two drawbridges, with large one-masted smacks that carried on the trade, both goods and passengers, between Leith and London. Above the upper bridge the shore was always lined with colliers, hence the name of Coalhill'.

'There were three or four Companies, to whom the smacks belonged; and it used to be an amusement to the denizens of Edinburgh and Leith to go down to see the smacks sail, as they usually did, three or four at a time on the Tuesdays and Fridays; and fine looking vessels they were, in latter times very handsomely fitted up for passengers. But their voyages were very wearisome. Fifty hours was reckoned a quick passage; but they oftener took a week or even considerably more.'

'Today the old harbour is all but empty of ships and vessels, not a craft at the Coalhill, and, between the bridges, only two small steam-tugs. All the smacks are gone, and even their successors, the clipper-schooners. Nothing has been able to withstand the steam; and the last sailing Company was dissolved two years ago.'

But look at the advertisements by the shipping companies in 1890 and see the destinations – Rotterdam, Amsterdam, Antwerp, Ghent, Dunkirk; tours to Norway; steam to Aberdeen (four times a week); Orkney and Shetland (thrice weekly); Leith to New York – regular steamers 'sail about every ten days'. It was boom time again. Street names such as Elbe, Baltic, Cadiz, Madeira and Antigua reflect the trading connections which Leith has always managed to maintain.

Now the docks are going through another period of adjustment – industry has been attracted by the Forth Ports Authority to replace the decline in ship traffic entering Leith: much is now oil-related and heads towards the Hound Point terminal off South Queensferry. Other companies in the oil business have found working space within the dockland, and sometimes a luxury passenger cruise ship or even a full-masted sailing ship brings a touch of the past glory days to the docks.

The possible development of the Water of Leith for other purposes taxed many brains, and as early as 1552 there is mention in the minutes of Edinburgh Town Council of a proposal to take the river into the North Loch, which lay below the Castle Rock where Princes Street Gardens are. In 1593 an Italian merchant called Marques put forward the suggestion of

Sometimes the visitors are regular navymen. This time they are minesweepers from the Royal Netherlands Navy who tied up during a naval exercise in 1988.

bringing the sea into the loch, and this was sent to a committee to be examined. Nothing more came of it.

Several other schemes for tapping the Water were put up, and in 1728 the Earl of Mar wanted to drive a branch from Coltbridge to run through the Nor' Loch 'which would be of great advantage of the convenience, beauty, cleanliness and healthiness of the town'.

When the Union Canal was being discussed at the end of the eighteenth century, grandiose schemes included taking it through the loch and forming a harbour basin at Greenside, with a canal linking it to the sea – a scheme which would hardly have appealed to the people of Leith, surely!

One proposal put forward about 1700 makes fascinating reading – 'A new and easy project of making the Water of Leith navigable; whereby ships may pass, and enter into the North Lough'. 'It requireth a very great Genius for Trade to overcome the Impediment of Local distance from the Sea Port, to have it flourishing. As this Canal when it is made will yield no small increase to Traders, having such a Commodious Port for their Commerce, so strangers will be encouraged to flock here with their Commodities, when they can so easily by Sea, enter into the Heart of a great City,' says the author.

He suggested that a ditch from the Shoar, 'where the Horse-courses are run', to the end of the Calton Hill might be possible, but because of likely building difficulties, he favoured making the channel of the Water of Leith deeper from the Bridge of Leith to Innerleith, 'and then cut through the Narrow Tract of land, from thence to the North-Lough, which must be made proportionately deep, to run in a straight level to the sea'.

He also proposed that the work could be done 'in a little space of time' by 300 men hewing a ditch 120 feet broad and 50 feet deep, mostly along the channel of the Water of Leith. He even reckoned the cost at £1583 6s. 8d. sterling, and envisaged stairs, wharves and quays from the banks above the Nor' Loch for loading and unloading the ships.

And lest there were objections from the old port, he added: 'The Commerce of the Town of Leith will not suffer by this New Canal: For beside that they have their own Harbour left entire to them; And they may still enjoy as much Sea Trade as they please; Tradesmen at Leith, as Sailmakers etc will still be receiving Profit by Ships that come up to Edinburgh'.

About 150 years later 'An Old Voyager' published a paper projecting a navigable river from Leith to Edinburgh as one way of eliminating the stagnant pools which were blamed for the cholera then prevalent. 'The only means that will ever effect a radical cure of the evils to be removed is to make the bottom of Leith Harbour and the bottom of the stream equally on a level up as high as Stockbridge. Measuring the serpentine course of the channel the distance proposed to be deepened is under two miles, and the ascent from the bottom of the Harbour to bed of the channel at Warriston Cemetery is little more than 25 feet, and at Stockbridge 50 feet.'

The Leith Dock Commission during the First World War appointed a special committee 'to consider the desirability of their taking action in regard to the movement now on foot for establishing deep water canal communications between the Firths of Forth and Clyde'.

In their report, printed on February 8, 1918, the committee said there had been 'intermittent agitation which has existed

A scene that is gone forever. The old Henry Robb's shipbuilding yard in the docks closed in 1983 despite a desperate fight by the much reduced workforce to save it. And with it went another of the old industries of Leith.

for upward of a generation' in favour of constructing such a canal, and their engineers believed that 'although no Canal is ever likely to be constructed across Scotland on a purely commercial basis, yet in their opinion the proposed Canal will have a commercial value that justifies the expectation of sufficient revenue from commercial vessels being secured ultimately to meet, at least, the cost of maintenance'.

The committee were told that their engineers estimated the cost of a direct route at £52,000,000 and an alternative line via Loch Lomond at £35,500,000, the direct line being fifty miles from deep water to deep water in both firths.

While Leith would be the 'greatest gainer' in the project, estimated to take between ten to sixteen years on the direct route to complete, the committee were not enthusiastic and felt costs would outweigh any savings in ships' time. They

LEITH AND NEW YORK.

REGULAR STEAMERS BETWEEN LEITH AND NEW YORK.

THE LARGE   FAST STEAMERS

'Croma,' 'Crystal,' 'Critic,' 'Mineola,' and 'Montauk,'

SAIL ABOUT EVERY TEN DAYS.

AGENTS:

HUGH BLAIK, Steamship Owners and Brokers, LEITH.

The halcyon days – from Leith to almost anywhere. The business with the Continent was fast and furious, and as this advertisement of 1890 shows, there was a regular service to New York.

expressed the view that 'the construction of the Canal ought not to be undertaken from any false idea of commercial prospects but only on the grounds of national necessity if the government should be so advised'.

Prior to the Second World War, the then City Treasurer, Will Y. Darling, suggested that 'paddling pools and yachting ponds' could be formed in the Water of Leith and fire fighting forces could draw supplies from them in the event of war – a move reminiscent of the early days of the municipal fire brigade who readily pumped water from the river whenever possible in their fire fighting.

Nowadays most of the stream is left unhampered by any form of transport for the anglers who benefit from the annual restocking of brown trout. Under the watchful eye of the Honorary Bailiffs of the Water of Leith, who are headed by a High Bailiff, the fishing is protected and encouraged, and to the casual observer enjoyed by anglers of all ages.

Leith has its own statue to Robert Burns, and Queen Victoria too. Scotland's bard wrote: 'The boat rocks at the pier o' Leith; Fu' loud the wind blaws frae the ferry. The ship rides by the Berwick Law, And I maun leave my bonnie Mary'.

Leith itself is going through a very welcome transformation with the Leith Project. Through huge investment, the Scottish Development Agency have encouraged an industrial, commercial and waterside housing revival. Particular attention was given by the agency's project team to the area at the Shore where by 1981 the problems of redundant buildings and dereliction were most acute.

The public impression of a run-down area had also to be overcome, and an extensive campaign to project a 'Leith-sur-Mer' image was generated, concentrating on cobbled waterfronts, dockside cafes and a general ambience of well-being and comfortable prosperity certainly round the Water.

New-style bistros and excellent restaurants vie with each other for custom, much of it from Edinburgh; the public houses benefit from the most liberal licensing laws in Britain; while the housing boom has brought people back into the area.

There is too a new awareness of the old port's archaeological heritage, and the Edinburgh District planning committee have designated as sites of special significance the original place of settlement – the area bounded by the Shore, Water Street, Broad Wynd and Tolbooth Wynd; and the North Leith riverbank, particularly between Coburg Street/Sandport Street and the Water of Leith. What subsequent research will reveal we will have to await.

A poem printed by John Moir in 1815 summed up Leith then:

> There's nothing stirring, nothing thro' the town
> But idle merchants loitering up and down;
> Wher'er we turn, some melancholy sign
> Appears, to mark stagnation and decline.

A pessimistic note, and that could have been Leith only a few years ago. But the poet's eye could see the future too:

> But better times, I hope, are now in store,
> The Forth again behold, with conscious pride,
> Whole fleets of merchantmen float on its tide;
> Commerce, and arts, and industry revive,
> And Leith with trade once more will be alive.

And through it all the 'majestic river' will float on, secure in its place in the history of a city and a town. A river whose working potential has been seized and utilised to the hilt, whose full potential for sheer pleasure has still to be fulfilled.

It is there to be discovered and enjoyed.

Further Reading

Patrick Abercrombie and Derek Plumstead, *A Civic Survey and Plan for Edinburgh*

Books of the Old Edinburgh Club

Malcolm Cant, *Villages of Edinburgh*, 2 vols. (1986 and 1987)

Robert Chambers, *Traditions of Edinburgh*

Alison Hay Dunlop, *Anent Old Edinburgh*

John Geddie, *The Water of Leith: Source to Sea*

James Grant, *Old and New Edinburgh*

Cumberland Hill, *Historic Memorials and Reminiscences of Stockbridge*

Stanley Jamieson, ed., *The Water of Leith*

J. C. Irons, *Leith and its Antiquities*

James Scott Marshall, *The Life and Times of Leith*

New Statistical Account of Scotland, Edinburgh (1845)

D. Robertson, *The Bailies of Leith*

John Russell, *The Story of Leith*

John Shaw, *Water Power in Scotland, 1550-1870* (1984)

Statistical Account of Scotland, Vol. II – The Lothians (1791-99)

James Steuart, *Notes for a History of Colinton Parish*

John Tweedie, *A Water of Leith Walk*

John Tweedie and Cyril Jones, *Our District*

A. J. Youngson, *The Making of Classical Edinburgh*

Index